Timothy Brecknock

# Droit le roy

A digest of the rights and prerogatives of the imperial crown of

Great-Britain

Timothy Brecknock

**Droit le roy**
*A digest of the rights and prerogatives of the imperial crown of Great-Britain*

ISBN/EAN: 9783337272098

Printed in Europe, USA, Canada, Australia, Japan

Cover: Foto ©Suzi / pixelio.de

More available books at **www.hansebooks.com**

# Droit le Roy.

Or a DIGEST of the

# RIGHTS and PREROGATIVES

OF THE

# IMPERIAL CROWN

OF

# *GREAT-BRITAIN.*

---

BY A MEMBER OF THE SOCIETY
OF *LINCOLN's-INN.*

---

DIEU ET Mon Droit.

---

LONDON:

Printed and Sold by W. GRIFFIN, in Fetter-Lane.

MDCCLXIV.

# INTRODUCTION.

SAINT Germain, in his Doctor and Student, a treatise most deservedly esteemed of the highest authority, observes, "That the third ground of the law of England standeth upon divers *general* customs, of old time used through all the realm, which have been accepted and approved by our Sovereign Lord the King, "and his progenitors, and *all* his subjects.

"And because the said customs be neither against the law of God, nor the law of reason, and have been *always* taken to be good and necessary for the common wealth of *all* the realm, therefore they have obtained the strength of a law in so much that he that doth act against them, doth act against justice; and these be the customs that properly be called the COMMON LAW."

The great lord Coke, speaking of the common law, saith, it is not only grounded upon reason, but it is the perfection of reason, acquired by long study, observation and experience, and refined by learned men in all ages: and I beg leave farther to add,

add, that it is the common parent of the subject's * liberties, and the king's prerogatives: both the one and the other deriving their very form and constitution from it.

I have been thus explicit in describing what the common law is, because I am thoroughly persuaded not one person in twenty of our clergy and gentry, nor one in ten thousand of our common people, know the distinction between *statute* and *common law*: and for want of this knowledge they have been lately led astray by strange notions of right and wrong, generally mistaking the one for the other. A mistake entirely owing, I hope, to their ignorance, for as they know not the various operations of our laws, they might easily imagine that what in one and the same case is binding to the people, should also be equally binding to the king: but *è contrario*, the common law having time immemorially prescribed to the sovereign and the subject a distinct peculiar circle of action, hath placed the prerogative royal in so super-eminent a station, that what is law almost in every

* By 25 Ed. 1. it is declared, that the *Great Charter* of liberties shall be taken as the *Common Law*.

caſe of the king, is law ſcarcely in any one caſe of the ſubject.

Two reaſons may be alledged for this almoſt-national ignorance of the common-law (ſo far I mean as it deſcribes and upholds the juſt rights of the crown.)

*Firſt*, becauſe the rights and liberties of the people, ever ſince the acceſſion of the houſe of Brunſwick, and in particular ſince the acceſſion of his preſent majeſty, to the imperial diadem of this realm, have been never diminiſhed, but frequently enlarged: witneſs, the ſeveral acts of parliament paſſed of late years "*for the further* LIMITATION *of the crown, and better ſecuring the rights and liberties of the people.*" Witneſs his preſent Majeſty's moſt gracious ſpeech, in 1760, from the throne to both houſes of parliament, when, unſollicited, and of his own mere godlike motion, he was pleaſed to declare, "That he looked upon the in-
" dependency and uprightneſs of Judges as
" eſſential to the impartial adminiſtration
" of juſtice, and as one of the beſt ſecuri-
" ties to the rights and liberties of his lov-
" ing ſubjects, and therefore recommend-
" ed it to the conſideration of his parlia-

" ment

" ment to make farther provision for con-
" tinuing judges in the enjoyment of their
" offices during their good behaviour,
" notwithstanding the demise of his ma-
" jesty, or any of his heirs and successors."
Witness also the grateful answer of both houses on this momentous occasion in the following express terms, "In return for your Majesty's paternal goodness, and in the justest sense of your tender concern for the religion, laws, and liberties of your people, we have taken this important work into consideration, and have resolved to enable your majesty to effectuate the wise, just, and generous purposes of your royal heart: any law, usage, or practice, to the contrary thereof in anywise notwithstanding."

The *second* cause of this amazing ignorance, in almost all degrees of persons, is owing to the difficulties attending the acquirement of a competent knowledge in this branch of literature: since it is but too notorious that the several laws and customs respecting the prerogative royal, are not collected in a masterly manner into one body, as our canon, statute, and mutiny laws are, but lye ſcattered and diſperſed amongſt the rubbiſh and lumber of our monkiſh hiſtories, Engliſh-Latin annals, Anglo-Saxon manuſcripts, Norman-French records, dull law-books, and parliamentary rolls.

Theſe, I take to be the two principal cauſes that the DROIT LE ROY has been ſo little underſtood this century even by men of letters and other gentlemen, whoſe duty it is either as eccleſiaſtic or civil magiſtrates not only to know it thoroughly themſelves, but early to inculcate and diffuſe its loyal principles amongſt their ſeveral neighbours, pariſhioners, and dependants: for on this law (which exalts our king ſo much above his ſubjects) depends that due ſubordination which conſtitutes the political beauty, harmony, and ſtrength of every well governed ſtate, and without which no ſtate whatever can long endure without ruſhing into anarchy and confuſion.

To render this moſt uſeful and requiſite knowledge more eaſily acquirable, the author of this treatiſe hath, with unwearied and intenſe application, collected from various yet authentic ſources of antiquity, the ſeveral ſcattered parts and formed them into one body or digest of the *Prerogative Royal*, and by so doing hath reduced that necessary learning within the narrow compass of two or three hours reading, which otherwise must have been the painful study and irksome fatigue of many years.

The author presumes not to arrogate to himself any other merit, but that of an indefatigable and faithful compiler: yet well knowing the great utility and necessity of such a work, he presumes to recommend a careful and frequent perusal of it to the bishops of every diocese, the lords-lieutenants of every county, the governors of every colony, the lords of trade and plantation, the lords commissioners of the board of admiralty, and in particular the secretaries of state, not doubting but their affection, loyalty, and zeal towards the most virtuous monarch that ever graced the British throne, will, like a secret charm, impel them diligently to distribute this little treatise to every one of the subordinate clergy, gentlemen in the commission of peace, and other civil officers, under their respective departments and jurisdictions: to the end that the dignity of the crown being universally understood, and the fundamental principles on which this pre-eminent dignity is *lawfully* founded being communicated by their influence and example throughout the whole Britiſh empire, every Great-Briton may be ſatisfactorily convinced that the *liberties* of the ſubject and the *prerogatives* of the king are conjunctives ſo conſtitutionally blended together in one joint intereſt, that ſpringing from one common parent (the great common law of the land) both the one and the other, like the two conjoined twins mentioned by Hippocrates, muſt neceſſarily rejoice or mourn, flouriſh or fade, exiſt or periſh together.

Laſtly, altho' we live in an age, in which the frivolty of French faſhions ſeems to be growing into ſovereign contempt with every ſenſible Great-Briton, the author cannot but think himſelf ſufficiently juſtifiable in prefixing the French title of *Droit le Roy* to this treatiſe; ſince of all the phraſes expreſſive of the *Prerogative Royal*, this ſeems to be the only one that correſponds with the motto to the royal arms of Great-Britain, Dieu et Mon Droit: a motto full of abſtruſe political learning, and by which

we

we are to underſtand that every monarch on the Britiſh throne is under an indiſpenſible obligation both to himſelf and his royal heirs, religiouſly to defend and maintain without impeachment of waſte, or the minuteſt diminution, "the abſolute "indefeaſible *ſupreamacy* over the Anglican church, the *ſovereign ſeignory* over "the empire of Great Britain and Ireland, "and the *hereditary right and title* to "the crown of France to its fulleſt extent;" and for this reaſon hath the royal motto, as a perpetual memento, been handed down in the *French language*, from the reign of Edward the THIRD, of glorious memory, to *that* of George the THIRD, our preſent virtuous and incomparable monarch, whom God long preſerve.

# DROIT Le ROY,

## OR, A

# Candid Aſſertion

## OF THE

# RIGHTS

## OF THE

## *Imperial Crown of* ENGLAND.

BEFORE we give a definition, or rather a deſcription of the autocratorical power and dominion appertaining to the kings of England, it will be neceſſary to preſent the readers with a view of the ſeveral appellations, which this power, has received by the Grecian, Roman, and our Engliſh lawyers.

The Grecians in their laws term it, Ἄκραν ἐξουσίαν, Κυρίαν Ἀρχὴν, Κύριον πολίτευμα, Αὐτοκρατορίαν, Ἐξουσίαν Αὐτοκρατορικὴν, Ἐξουσίαν ὑπερέχουσαν, Ἐξουσίαν Ἀρχιτεκτονικὴν, Ἐξῃρημένην Αἰτίαν, πρῶτον Ἀξίωμα, Δύναμιν Ἀναγκαστικὴν.

The Civilians call it, *Summum imperium, jura imperii, ſummi imperii jus, jura majeſtatis regiæ, majeſtatis imperium, majeſtatem, imperii majeſtatem, majeſtatem principis ſupremam, ſacra regni, regalia, ſummum imperii, ſummum arbitrium, ſacra ſacrorum,*



*dignitatis*

*dignitatis praeminentiam, supremam potestatem, potestatem summam, potestatem supereminentem, imperii potestatem, authoritatem supremam, supremitatem, sereniffimam majestatem regiam.*

The appellations among us are fuch as thefe, *Privilegium regis, jus regium, jus regium coronæ, dreit le roy, royalty, regality, royal authority, royal eftate, privilege royal, fovereign feigniory, royal dominion, feigniory royal, imperial majefty, the royal eftate of the imperial crown, the imperial crown of England, fovereign and royal authority, fovereignty, fupremacy, prebeminence royal, prerogative royal,* and the like.—But the reader call it what he pleafes, I thus defcribe it.

It is the exempt, abfolute and independent power, the fupreme dignity of England, that acknowledgeth no fuperior, but God Almighty, not to be divided, communicated, nor transferred to any perfon whatfoever. Out of this defcription thefe four maxims may be deduced.

1. *That the kings of England did never* de jure *acknowledge any fuperior here on earth, either in church or ftate.*
2. *That the fovereignty of England is indivifible.*
3. *That the regality of this realm is incommunicable.*
4. *That the royalty of England is unalienable.*

These four deductions fhall be made good by feveral authorities.

1. *That the kings of England did never acknowledge any fuperior here on earth, either in church or ftate.*

IT is reported, that when Sigifmond the emperor, cozen-german to the moft victorious prince king Henry the fifth, accompanied with the arch-bifhop of Rhemes, ambaffador from the French king, arrived at Calis, to whom were fent feveral great fhips to waft him over: at Dover, the duke of Gloucefter, with a brave company of gallants, (upon the emperor's approaching to land) with their fwords drawn, ftept up to their knees in water, protefting, *If he came as the king's friend, or for his honour to move ought, he fhould be welcome; but if as an emperor he claimed any jurisdiction,*

*tion, they were ready to resist him to the last drop of their blood.* Upon this declaration, the emperor renounced all imperial authority, jurisdiction and sovereignty: and with great reason; for the regality of this nation was never *de jure* attendant to any foreign prince or potentate; but was ever imperial, exempt, absolute, independant, subject to none but God, equivalent to that power which any supreme prince whatever, has at any time, in any part of the world, (of right) challenged to himself; and this assertion will be apparented by these authorities following: first, to begin with the statute laws, not as new introductive laws, but as explanatory revivers of the old common law of this land.

Note, that our king, whose government is politic, is of no less power than he that royally ruleth his people after his own pleasure, although they differ in authority over their subjects. *Fortescue* c. 11.

In 16. R. 2. it is declared, *That the crown of England hath been free at all times; that it hath been in no earthly subjection, but immediately subject to God in all things touching the regality to the same crown, and none other.* 16 R. 2. chap. 5.

In 24 Hen. 8. It is resolved, declared, and recognized, *That by sundry old authentic histories and chronicles, it is manifestly declared and exprest, that this realm of England is an empire, and so has been reputed in the world.* 24 H. 8. chap. 21.

In the 25th H. 8. it is declared, *That this realm, recognizing no superior under God, but only the king, hath been, and is free from subjection to any man's laws*; but only to such as have been devised and obtained within this realm for the wealth of the same, or to such other as by sufferance of his GRACE, and his progenitors, the people have taken at their free liberty, by their own consent to be used among them. 25 H. 8. chap. 21.

In the first year of queen Elizabeth, it is reported, *That the crown of England is imperial. After statutes,* it may be also apparented from our antient authors in the law. 1 Eliz. chap. 1.

Lib. 1. c. 8. num. 5. *Omnis sub rege*, (says Bracton) *& ipse sub nullo, nisi tantum sub Deo. Parem autem non habet in regno suo, quia sic amitteret præceptum, cum par in parem non habeat imperium.* With Bracton concurs our *Fleta. lib.* 1. c. 5.

Mirror. c. 1. sect. 2. *Le Roy ne devoit aver nul peer en sa terre.*

Co. 4. Instit 342. Rot. claus. 13. Ed. 2. m. 6. Public Notaries, made by the emperor, claimed to exercise their office here in England, but were prohibited, because it was against the dignity of a supreme king.

Cambden's Britania, f. 163, in Engl. The king, (saith Cambden), hath sovereign power, and absolute command among us, neither holdeth he his empire in vassalage, nor receiveth the investiture, or installing from another, nor yet acknowledgeth any superior but God alone.

Sir John Davy's reports. Le case deil county palat. 61. a. Upon a difference arising betwixt king William the second, and Anselme, arch-bishop of Canterbury, touching the jurisdiction and authority of the bishop of Rome; the king alledged, *That none of his bishops ought to be subject to the pope; but the pope himself ought to be subject to the emperor, and that the king of England had the same absolute liberty in his dominions, as the emperor had in his empire.*

Davis's reports le case dell count. palat. 60. B. The doctors of the imperial law hold, *Quod solus princeps, qui est monarcha & imperator in regno suo, ex plenitudine potestatis, potest creare comitem Palatinum.*

The kings of England have made counties palatine, as the counties palatine of Lancaster, Chester, Durham, and Pembroke, and granted them royal rights and privileges; and therefore the king of England is an absolute monarch within his dominions and territories.

Bracton, lib. 3. c. 9. de actionibus, co. 3. inst. 57. dr. & stu. lib. 2. c. 51 Co. Lit. 65 Beverlies To be short, the king is stiled in our books of law, God's vicar on earth, God's lieutenant, *pater patriæ, supremus Dominus*, lord paramont, *nostre Signior le Roy*, &c. &c. &c.

a. Co. 2. Inst. 273r Lit sect. 85, 87. 153, 159. Co. lib. 4. case west. 1. C. 17. Co. lib. 9. 38. B.

By

By the foregoing conſtats, it appears clearly, that the monarchy of England is an abſolute, free, and independent regality, recognizing no ſuperior on earth, but God Almighty.

It is alſo evident by our books of Law, that the king of England is abſolute and ſupreme lord of Scotland, Wales and Ireland. And,

## 1. *Of* SCOTLAND.

THE kings of England had ever appertaining to them, the ſuperior dominion of Scotland, as ſhall be manifeſted by theſe authorities following: the Scots performed the oath of fidelity and homage, to Edred king of England; Kennethus king of Scots, did homage to our king Edgar; and Conſtantine the Scottiſh king yielded homage and allegiance to Athelſtan, king of England.

Malcolme king of Scots, to William the conqueror; Duncan the ſon of Malcolme, to William Rufus; David of Scotland to Matilda the empreſs, (daughter to H. 1.) and for this cauſe the ſame David being required by king Stephen to do his homage, refuſed; becauſe he had already done it to the empreſs Matilda; but Henry, the ſon of David, performed it to our king Stephen, and Malcolme king of Scots, to our Henry the ſecond; William king of Scots to our king John; Alexander the Scottiſh king, to Henry the third; and to Edward the firſt, kings of England.

Alexander dying without iſſue, John Balliol, and David Bruce, contending for the ſucceſſion, the peers of Scotland referred the controverſy to our king Edward the firſt, as their ſupreme lord and judge; and by virtue of this ſupremacy and ſuperiority over that nation, Balliol was conſtituted king of Scotland.

After the defeat of Hallidown-hill, Balliol king of Scots, at Newcaſtle, did homage to E. 3. king of England, as his ſuperior lord, and takes his oath of fealty, binding himſelf and his heirs, to hold that kingdom of him and his ſucceſſors for ever.

Humfrey duke of Glouceſter, protector to king H. 6. H 6.
ranſomed and enlarged the king of Scots, (who had been for many years priſoner) taking homage and fealty of him for the crown of Scotland, the form and inſtrument of this homage

homage I will transcribe, verbatim as I find it recorded. "*I James Steward, king of Scots, shall be true and* "*faithful unto our lord H. by the grace of God, king of* "*England and France, the noble and superior lord of* "*Scotland, and to you I make my fidelity for the same* "*kingdom, which I hold and claim of you; and I shall* "*bear you faith and fidelity, of life and limb, and* "*worldly honour against all men, and faithfully I shall* "*acknowledge, and shall do you service due for the* "*kingdom of England aforesaid: So God me help.*"

Cap. 13. vide Selden's notes on this chap. To conclude with justice Fortescue, who tells us, that Scotland was subject to England, as a dukedom, and was after advanced to a politic and royal kingdom.

And, more may be found touching England's superiority over the kingdom of Scotland, in these authors following: Dr. Duck, lib. 2. c. 10. *De authoritate Juris civilis Romanorum.* Matthew Paris, Daniel's history, and Trussel's history of H. 6. Camb. Eliz. *Anno* 1560. Lord Herbert's H. 8. p. 481. 1 H. 7. 10. a.

## 2. *Of* Wales.

THE kings of England were ever supreme lords of Wales, as appears by these vouchers:

Co. 3 inst. fol. 11. Co 2. inst. on stat. west. 1. David prince of Wales, levied war against Edw. 1. this was treason, by reason, that David was within the homage and legiance of the king of England, and judgment was accordingly given against him as a traitor, and not as an enemy.

27 H. 8. c. 26. It was declared, in the 27th year of H. 8. that the king's most royal majesty, of meer Droit, and very right, is very head, king, and lord, and ruler of Wales.

## 3. *Of* Ireland.

Co. 4. inst. 359. THAT the king of England is absolute and supreme lord of Ireland, is manifested so early as in the reign of king Edgar, who, by his charter of Oswald's law, deprived the married priests, and introduced the monks; this instrument is dated at Glocester 966.

The next account we find of our king's having sovereign authority over Ireland, is in the reign of Henry 2.

ry 2. for upon that king's landing at Waterford, and staying there a few days, *rex Corcagiensis Dermitius*, (saith *Giraldus Cambrensis*, who was secretary and historiographer to Hen. 2d. and accompanied him in his expedition into Ireland) *advenit ei, et tam Subjectionis Vinculo quam Fidelitatis Sacramento regi anglorum se sponte submisit.* He voluntarily swore fealty and subjection to the king of England. The same author farther observes, that on Henry's arrival at Cashel, Dunaldus, king of Limerick, *se quoque fidelem regi exhibuit:* together with all the nobility and princes in the south of Ireland: and also on his arrival at Dublin, that Macshaglin, king of Ophaly, O'Carrol, king of Urich, O'Rourk, king of Meath, Rotheric O'Conner, king of Connaught, and as it were monarch of the whole Island, came in, *et firmissimis fidelitatis et subjectionis vinculis Domino Regi se innodarunt.* This account is likewise authenticated by the annalist Roger Hovedon (*vide annal. Parsposter fol.* 301.) About the kalends of November, saith he, king Henry 2d. of England, landed at Waterford, *et sibi venerunt ad eum rex Corcagiencis, rex de Limeric, rex de Oxenie, rex Mediæ, omnes archepiscopi, episcopi et abbates totius Hiberniæ, et receperunt eum in Regem & Dominum Hiberniæ jurantes ei et hæreditus suis fidelitatem, et Regnandi super eos potestatem in perpetuum.* Mathew Paris, speaking to the same effect, saith, *ipsum Henricum in Regem et Dominum receperunt, et ei fidelitatem & homagium juraverunt.* John Brampton, abbot of Jornal, in his *Historia Jornalensi* p. 1070, speaking of the several kings, princes, archbishops, &c. of Ireland, saith, that king Henry received from every one of them, *litteras cum sigillis in modum chartæ pendentibus regnum Hiberniæ sibi et hæredibis suis confirmantes, et testimonium perhibentes ipso in Hiberniâ eum et hæredes suos sibi in Reges et Domines in perpetuum constituisse.* Thus it is evident from these extracts, that Henry 2d. and our other king's of England, were in fact, kings of Ireland, although they only stiled themselves Lords of that kingdom, 'till the 33d. of Henry 8th. when that monarch took the stile and title of King of Ireland.

But after all these confirmations, the reader may say, that he was long ago very well satisfied concerning the king of England's superiority over Scotland, Wales and

and Ireland; but he would be glad to know what title the king has to the realm of France: and the rather, becaufe we give him the title of king of France, in all our inftruments, &c.

'Tis anfwered, that our king has a juft and a legal title to that kingdom, upon the account of Edward 3. king of England, whofe title to the crown of France is agreed to by all hiftorians to be thus:

Philip the 4th. called Philip le Bell, eldeft brother to Charles de Valois, married Johan, queen of Navar, and by her had three fons,

Lovis, fir-named Hutin or Mutineer, Philip the Long, and Charles the Fair, and one daughter named Ifabella, that was married to king Edward 2. king of England, and furvived her three brothers, who died every one of them without iffue of their bodies lawfully begotten.

Thefe fucceffively, one after another, had enjoyed the crown of France; but after the death of the third brother Charles, a pretended fundamental law of that kingdom, (called The Law Salique) excluding women from fovereign inheritance was broached by Philip of Valois, fon of Charles the younger, brother to Philip le Bell, who endeavouring to put the Salique Law in execution, laid hold of the crown, againft whom, in the right of his mother Ifabella, our king Edward 3. oppofing and quartering the arms of France, which was Semi de Luces, proclaimed his title to be king of France and England, and in hoftile manner entered France with banners difplayed, where he performed fuch marvellous exploits, that whilft any records laft, cannot be forgotten.

There he continued victorious during the time of Valois, and left his fon the Black Prince, to profecute the claim, who, to his eternal honour, took not only John, the French king prifoner, but braved Charles 5. to his teeth unanfwered, that wife king thinking it no good policy to meet a roaring lion in the field. Since
H. 5. Edward 3d. time, our king Henry 5. advanced his banner, and challenged the fame rightful fovereign inheritance, and proved moft fortunately victorious.

H. 6. Upon the fame account H. 6. was crowned at Paris, king of France, receiving the oaths of homage and fealty, of all the nobility of France prefent, and of all the

the citizens and inhabitants of that city, and the places adjacent.

Having presented to the reader a survey of our king's title to the crown of France, it will not be impertinent that the validity of this pretended Salique Law be now inquisited and examined.

The pretended Salique Law is this, *That the crown shall descend to the next heir male, and exclude all females.*

The unjust surmise of this same law, I shall endeavour to refell, both by reason and examples.

1. By reason, *in terram salicam mulieres ne succedant*, is the text on which the French build this law; I say, this law was made in Germany, to discountenance the dishonest manners of the German women, and had no relation to France: for Pharamond, whom the French affirm to be the author of this constitution, deceased above three hundred and fifty years before the French were placed beyond the river Sala; the one dying at four hundred twenty-six, and the other being seated there *Anno* 805. Now, let any man that understands the nature and import of a positive law, judge whether there be any colour of reason in this extravagant solution: *for a law is the direction of the person that governeth, to be observed by those that are governed.* How then can the Gallican crown devolve, or descend according to the custom of the Salians, if the French crown be not subject to the people of Salia? but where this country of Salia should be, no geographer or historian, ancient or modern can tell us.

2. As for examples—we will cite amongst others, Pepin, Hugh Capet, and Lewis 9. who enjoyed the French crown, not by virtue of the Salique law, but as heirs generally, or otherways.

First for Pepin; he having put Childerick into a monastery, had not any colour of title, but as he was chosen by the parliament of Paris; so that it seems the parliament of Paris may do what the king and general-assembly cannot, and alter the most fundamental constitution of France, which at other times is immutable, not to be altered by the king, and states-general.

Secondly, for Hugh Capet, who, to make his title good against Charles of Lorain, the right Masculin heir to Pepin, did derive his pedigree from one of the Daughters of Charlemain, son of king Pepin.

Thirdly, for Lewis 9. He (a most religious prince) could not be resolved in conscience to take upon him the government, untill he was satisfied, that by his grand-mother's side, he was descended from the right heirs of Charles of Lorain. In short, I admire with what confidence the French can urge this law against others, and yet practice the contrary themselves. As for instance, Charles the eighth, having married Claude the dutchess of Britain, (and by that title possessed the dutchy) by whom he had Claude, married to Francis the first, who had issue H. 2. that had issue Francis 2. Charles 9. H. 3. and Hercules, and Elizabeth married to Philip 2. of Spain, and Margaret to H. 4. Now Francis, Charles, Henry and Hercules, dying all without issue legitimate; we Englishmen would fain know, how, against the Salique Law, Charles and his posterity should have a title to Britain, and yet king Philip and his posterity, be debarred of it, by virtue of this pretended Salique Law.

For a conclusion to what I have said, touching the validity of this pretended French Salique Law; I shall subjoin the sentiments of Sir Thomas Ridley, in his view of the civil and ecclesiastical law, part 2. c. 1. sect. 8. And he has been pleased thus to express himself.

'Succession in kingdoms, says he, in most part of 'the world, in former time hath been, and at this 'day is, by right of blood (a few only excepted, which 'are elective, as the kingdom of Poland is at this day). 'And in succession, the eldest son taketh place before 'the rest; and if there be no heir male, then the 'eldest daughter succeedeth in the kingdom, and her 'issue; for kingdoms (as also succession in other dignities) are impartible. And yet France (to exclude 'Ed. 3. from the inheritance of the crown thereof, 'who descended of Isabel, the sister of Charles the fair, 'and so was next heir male to the crown of France), 'alledged for themselves the law Salique, pretending 'none, who claimed by the woman, albeit, he 'was the next heir male in blood, was to succeed, as 'long as there were of the male line alive; how far 'soever they were off, in degree from the last king 'deceased.

'deceased. But this is but a meer device of the 'French, fathered upon some rotten Record of that 'part of the gallic nation, called Salii, of whom other-'wise they have nothing memorable to speak of, as 'being the basest nation among them ll, of whom 'they report their people to have been compounded; 'but this device served their turn then, whether it 'were antiently invented, or newly coined.'

Thus much for the title that our kings have to Scotland, Wales, Ireland and France. To proceed now to my second deduction; that the regality of this realm will suffer no division.

## 2. *That the sovereignty of* England *is indivisible.*

THE dignity royal of this realm will not endure divisibility: as it will comport no superior, so it will admit no competitor. The world may as soon be governed by two suns, as this kingdom by several supreme legislators: for royal dominion is a plenitude, *quæ non capit plures in solidum.*

The royal dignity of a king or monarch, (says Coke) from which fountain all other subordinate dignities are deduced, *tanquam lumen de lumine*, are derived without any diminution, will suffer no division, *regia dignitas est indivisibilis.* Co.4.inst. 24.

Again, (says Coke) the dignity of the crown of England, is without all question descendable to the eldest daughter alone, and to her posterity, and so it hath been declared by act of parliament: for *regnum non est divisibile.* Co. Lit. 165. a. 25 H. 8. 22.

Moreover, let the reader review and consider all politicians, and they will grant, that *suprema potestas est in indivisibili posita*, supremacy and sovereignty is an indivisible and undivided entity. How can we share it then amongst more or many?

Besides, that the sovereignty of England, is an entity undivisible, I shall offer to prove by arguments, on the following *dilemma.*

Though government, for example, differs in *specie*, *viz.* Monarchy, Aristocracy, and Democracy, yet in all of them this power or command is the same and equal, *viz.* Supreme; and this power or command must reside in one object or one being, *viz.* in one

Man, in one Court, in one People: but if it be divided into two or more, it is either *supervacaneous* or *destructive:* for those two or more, in whom this divided empire doth consist, must either agree or disagree in the same thing; if they agree to will or nill the same, then it is supervacaneous: for it had been all one, if but one part had willed it, and *frustra fit per plura*, &c. but if they disagree in willing or nilling the same thing, it is destructive. For it is impossible for the subject to obey, because the law itself is a contradiction, and if the subject obeys one, he disobeys the other, and to obey neither, brings Anarchy and confusion upon all the governed: what is left then but the subject to be divided, as well as the power. And a 'kingdom divided in itself cannot stand;' neither are the governors in whom this divided power or command does consist, in any better case than the subject: for,

*Nulla fides regni sociis, omnisque potestas*
*Impatiens consortis erit.*——— Lucan.

This same argument, the Papalini would fain evade with a distinction of theirs; they tell us, that causes are two fold, spiritual and temporal; though neither the sovereignty in *temporalibus*, nor the supremacy in *spiritualibus* is impartible, not to be divided into two or more, yet the sovereignty may be vested in one person, as in the king; and the supremacy in another, as in the pope: so that the king shall be sovereign in matters secular, and the pope, supreme head in causes spiritual and ecclesiastical.

This is a distinction (say we) without a diversity; for the king of England as king, is supreme governor as well in causes spiritual, as in matters civil; the sovereignty of England, being a replete compacted body, and impartible. If the church interfere, and clash with the state, and struggle for a joint partnership, how can the scepter continue its prerogative, or the people their privileges? in a word, the spiritual and temporal authority are (and ought always to be) wreathed in the imperial crown, or it will not be worth wearing.

If what I have said, be not sufficient towards the confusion of this popish distinction, let the reader read the

the case of *Præmunire* in Sir. John Davis, his Irish Reports, and I am confident, he will judge it a meer vanity, a Chimera, or fantastical nothing, fit to be sent to purgatory for a token.

As for our Miso-monarchical sectaries, they endeavour to extricate themselves out of this Dilemma, by intoxicating the vulgar, with a new state-devised principle, *viz* that in monarchy, *the legislative power is communicable to the subject, and is not radically in soveraignty in one but in more*; so that that they fancy a *mixture* or *co-ordination*, in the very *supremacy* itself; that the *monarchy*, or highest power itself is compounded of three *co-ordinate* estates; and this some call a *mixt monarchy*. The vanity of which government will be evidenced by these following arguments:

The first is this, *monarchy* compounded of three *co-ordinate* estates, in plain English speaks this *nonsense*, the power which one only hath, is in three jointly and equally.

The second shall be this: if there be a *co-ordination* in the *supremacy*; that is, if our king, the lords and commons, are jointly, the supreme governor, the *correlatum* is wanting, none are left over whom they should reign, we should have a kingdom without a subject, because all may challenge a share in the soveraignty.

The third and last argument may be this, all agree that there are three sorts of government, Monarchy, Aristocracy and Democracy; now if they may be mixed, then sure there may be more than three, *viz.* Monarchy, Aristocracy and Democracy; Monarchy mixed with Aristocracy; Monarchy mixed with Democracy, and Monarchy mixed both with Aristocracy and Democracy: Aristocracy mixed with Monarchy, Aristocracy mixed with Democracy, and Aristocracy mixed with both. And so Democracy mixed with Monarchy, Aristocracy and both; so that either these three sorts of government will admit of no mixture, or else there may be above three sorts of regiment; and what must this government be called? could any person give a name to it, it must be either Aristomonarchy or Demonarchy: in plain English, the chief men-government of one man alone, or the people-government of one alone.

Having

Having given the reader my arguments to discover the deception and weakness of this Antimonarchical principle, which on this mixture or co-ordination, in the very supremacy of power itself is grounded, I will demonstrate the true meaning of that, which our new statists call a Mixt Monarchy.

Mr. Dudley Diggs.

If we speak correctly, there cannot be such a thing as *mixtum imperium*, a mixt manarchy, or a mixt Aristocracy, or mixt democracy; because, if there are divers supreme powers, it is no longer one state. If the supreme power be but one, and that authority be *le dernire resort de la justice*, or unto which the last appeal must be made, and against whose sentence, though unjust, we have not any legal remedy. This must be placed either in one person who is the fountain of all jurisdiction, and then it is a Monarchial government, or in some nobles, and then the regiment is Aristocratical, and the sentence of the major part of them becomes law to all effects, whether concerning our goods or lives: or if the civil constitutions of a state, direct us to appeal to the people, this is an absolute and true Democracy. By a mixt monarchy, therefore (not to quarrel about words) nothing but this position can rea-reasonably be understood, that it is not Παμβασιλεία, or Παντελὴς μοναρχία, in which the will of the prince publicly made known, gives the law, *quodqunque principi placet, legis habet vigorem*; but Βασιλεία κατὰ νόμον, a government not arbitrary, but restrained by positive constitutions, in which a prince hath limited himself by promise or oath, not to exercise full power. This grant is of force, because any man may either totally resign, or diminish his rights by covenant. Hence it is, that in monarchies all kings have supreme power, though they have not all the same *jura regalia*; their prerogatives are larger or narrower, according to their particular grants. For example, our kings have retained to themselves the rights of coining money, making great officers, bestowing honours, as dukedoms, baronies, knighthoods, &c. pardoning all offences against the crown, making war and peace, sending ambassadors to negotiate with foreign states, &c. and they have restrained themselves from the use of that power, which makes new laws, and repeals old, without the consent of the lords and commons in parliament, as likewise

likewise from raising money on the subject, without their consent.

More may be seen for the further discovery of this cheat; I mean, our new statist's mixture of government, in Mr. Roger Coke's observation on Mr. Whites Grounds, pag. 20, 21. Dr. Ferne, in his tract, entitled Conscience satisfied, sect. 4. In Sir Robert Filmer's two pieces, and in a treatise, entitled *Sacro-sancta Regum Majestas*, cap. 8. pag. 95. cap. 9. pag. 103. cap. 10. pag. 105. This last piece was printed in the year 1644, and dedicated to the marquiss, afterwards duke of Ormond.

### 3. *That regality of this realm is incommunicable.*

UNUM *imperium* (says Tacitus) *unius animo regendum est*; councel may be in many, as the senses, but the supreme power can be but in one, as the head; and therefore, neither it, nor any of its essential attributes can be totally communicated to any subject. As for example;

The king cannot grant power to any subject to pardon a felon; because it is a *prerogative* which is not grantable. 1H.4.5b.

So a corporation is a thing which ought to be instituted by the king himself, and by his own words, and therefore he cannot give licence to another to make a corporation. 2H.7.13. a.

So the king cannot grant to any other person, to make of Aliens born, Denizens; because, it is by the law inseparably and individually annexed to his royal person, and is a high point of royal prerogative. Co. lib.7. Calvin's Case.

Bracton tells us, *that the rights of the crown cannot be granted away. Those things which belong to jurisdiction and peace, and those things which are annexed to justice, appertain to none but to the crown and dignity of the king; nor can be separated from the crown; nor be possessed by any private person.* Lib. 2. c. 24. num 1.

The king cannot grant to me, to make my justices of peace, no more than he can grant to me the pardoning of felons: for he is the Chief Justice, and 'tis annext to his person, from which it cannot be severed. 20 H. 7. f. 7.a.S.a.

But after all this, it may be objected, that the chief governor of counties palatine had *jura regalia*, as fully

as

as the king had in his palace (for they could pardon treasons, murders, felonies, and outlawries. They [Co.4.inst. 20.] could make justices of eyre, justices of assize, of gaol-deliveries, and of the peace, *&c.*) And therefore sovereign power, and the essences seem to be communicable to subjects.

To this objection, this answer may be returned, that the power and authority of those that had counties palatine, was *de facto*, king-like; but this kingly power was afterwards resumed from them, and united [27 H.8.c. 24.] again to the crown, by the statute of 27 H. 8. if not for the illegality of the communicativeness, yet for the inconveniencies that arose from such communication; and yet, whilst these earls palatine had royal authority in all things, there was an acknowledgement of the king to be their superior lord and sovereign. [Lib. 3. c. 8. de Corona.] And so says Bracton, *comites palatini regalem habent potestatem in omnibus, salvo domino regi sicut principi.*

The sum of all is this, his majesty's prerogatives are as the lawyers speak, *in indivisibili posita quæ distrahi non possunt, minui non possunt*, are so indivisible in themselves, and naturally and intrinsically inherent in the crown, in his sovereignty and supremacy, that they cannot be made away; or so communicated to the subject, *ut defluat radix supremæ potestatis*, to devest himself of them, *ad minuendam majestatem* to lessen sovereign majesty, although, by trust and delegate power, the execution may be entrusted to others, *ad minuendam solicitudinem*, to ease him of unsupportable burthen. These essential attributes of sovereign power, are fitly resembled by the royal crown, from which, if you take away the least part, you spoil it so in its nature and shape, that it is no more a crown.

### 4. *That the Royalty of* England *is unalienable.*

BY the laws of this realm, it is not in the power of the king to collate his crown by any dispositive or testamentary will, or by any other act, the right descending to the next of blood, only by the custom and law of the kingdom; and therefore it hath been declared by the lords and commons, in parliament, [14.] *that no king can put himself, nor his realm, nor his people in subjection to any other potentate, without the assent of of the lords and commons in parliament; wherefore if king John had surrendred his kingdoms of England and Ireland, to the pope, by the common council of the barons, as his charter purported, yet it bound not; for it was not done in parliament by the king, lords, and commons. And albeit it might (as it appeareth, it cannot be done without authority of parliament), yet this is* contra legem & consuetudinem parliamenti *to do such a thing.* Roys ausi (*says our ancient Britton*) ne purront rien aliener en droit de lour corone, ne lour royaltie, que il ne soit repealeable, pur lour successors. Cap. 34. de Donus.

More of this learning may be seen in *Grot. lib.* 2. *c.* 7. *nu.* 25. *de jure Belli & Pacis.* 1 *H.* 7. 10. *a. Co. lib.* 12. *f.* 28. *Cowels inst.* 2. 8. *Swinburn's tract of Wills. Dr. Ducke lib.* 2. *c.* 9. *nu.* 5. *de authoritate juris civilis. Dr. Zouch pars* 1. *sect.* 3. *nu.* 2. *de jure inter gentes. pars* 2. *sect.* 7. *de juditio inter gentes.*

Agreeable to this doctrine, I positively affirm, that no king of England, (the English monarchy being by ancient custom, and fundamental laws of the realm, merely successive, either to the heirs male, or heirs general) can any ways dispose of this kingdom in prejudice to the next heir in blood, according to the custom, (I mean, male or general) no not though the parties interessed in the succession should commit treason, or should be excluded, by act of the states or parliament.

That treason cannot avoid a lawful succession in blood, we have an example in our king H. 7. who stood attainted of high treason, at the time of his coming into England, and yet no reversal of the attainder was made; for all the judges of England (after communication had amongst themselves) did agree, that the king was a person able, and discharged of any former attainder *ipso facto*, the moment he took upon him to reign, and to be king; and the reason then given was, because the imperial crown once worn, quite taketh away all defects. 1 *H.* 7. 4. *b. Plowd. Comment.* 225. *Co. Litt. f.* 16. *b.* lord Bacons, *H.* 7. *anno primo, & Cambd. Eliz. anno* 1559. Thus it manifestly (by the way) appeareth, that by the laws of England, there can be no *inter-regnum* within this kingdom, and that by discent, the next heir in blood is immediately compleatly and absolutely king, without any essential ceremony, Co. lib. 7. Calvin's case, Hil. 1. Jac. Regis in case of Watson and Clark popish priests, Co. 3. just. f. 7.

remony, or act to be done *ex post facto*, and that the coronation is but a royal ornament, and outward solemnization of the discent; a ceremony to shew the king unto the people. That is to say, coronation is only a ceremony, and such a ceremony as *doth* not any thing, but only declareth what is *done*: the king was king before it, as much as he is after it; only by it he is declared to be what he was before, and what he should have been still, though he had not been so declared. I pray you, what solemnity was used at the coronation of king James in Scotland? for he was crowned in the cradle, and by a people, who had profanely banished all manner of ceremonies, *Sedè diverticulo in viam*.

But, whether an act of Parliament may exclude the succession in blood, is the greatest question. And we for our parts have statutes that make it treason to deny it, but never otherwise made than only for fear or flattery of the present prince, and never observed; in the civil wars between the two houses of York and Lancaster, how many statutes have been made to the disinherison of the title of York, and all vanished in smoak?

The statute of 25 H. 8. c. 22. in disherison of queen Mary, and confirmed by another statute of 26 H. 8. c. 2 . how were they, I pray observed? and lastly, the great act of 35 H. 8. c. 1. which gave authority to the king, in case his own line should become extinct, to dispose of the kingdom, either under his great seal, or by will; have we not seen it, to the great and unspeakable joy of us all, most happily neglected so far, as that the very case, which in that statute is put, of the extinguishment of H. 8. his line, and a will made, such as it was, to the disinherison of the Scottish line, the validity of it was never so much as once considered upon by our council and lords, for it was wholly immaterial, whether the will was a will or not, since the act of itself was a void act that should have given strength to the will.

To what I have said, touching succession in hereditary monarchies, I shall presume to add the oppinion of two most learned and ingenius authors; namely, Mr. Roger Coke, and the late earl of Clarendon.

The former has these very words, 'No human law 'can create a human right, *jura sanguinis nullo jure*

'*civili*

'*civili dirivati possint*; nor is this right of succession 'from divine positive laws, but observed as well where 'God's revelation of himself is not received, as where 'it is; and if according to the resolution of all the 'most learned and reverend judges in Calvin's case, 'subjection is from no human law, but from the law 'of nature, then of necessity must regal right, and in'heritance be from the law of nature; for no man sup'poseth subjection where he does not presuppose power. 'The will therefore of Hen. 8. where for want of 'issue of Edward, Mary and Eliz. he gives the *Eng'lish* monarchy to the issue of Frances, and Elianor, 'daughters of Mary his younger sister, before the 'right heirs of Margaret, his eldest sister, wife of 'James the fourth of Scotland, was void, and not to 'be allowed; and so was that of Edward 6. who 'disinherited his sisters, Mary and Elizabeth, and gave 'the crown to Jane, daughter of Frances the French 'queen aforesaid, by Charles Brandon, duke of Suf'folk, and so were the acts of parliament made by 'H. 4. H. 5. & H. 6. which intailed the crown upon 'their heirs, so were the acts of Henry 6. which 'intailed the crown upon him and his heirs males of 'his body; and so were the acts of the 1 of R. 3. & 'H. 7. which intailed the crown upon them, and their 'heirs. Neither is succession and inheritance of crowns 'declared by any human law in the world, that I 'know of, but only the pretended French Salique 'law.'

The Earl of Clarendon, in his survey of the dangerous errors of church and state, in Mr. Hobs's book, intitled, *Leviathan*, pag. 61, expresseth himself thus:

'Methinks his own natural fear of danger, which 'made him fly out of France, as soon as his *Leviathan* 'was published, and brought into that kingdom, should have terrified him from invading the right of 'all hereditary monarchies in the world, by declaring, 'that by the law of nature which is immutable, it is 'in the power of the present sovereign to dispose of the 'succession, and to appoint who shall succeed him in 'the government; and that the word (heir) doth not 'of itself imply the children, or nearest kindred of a 'man; but whomsoever a man shall any way declare 'he wou'd have ſucceed him, contrary to the known 'right and eſtabliſhment throughout the world, and 'which would ſhake, if not diſſolve, the peace of all 'kingdoms.'

Thus much may ſuffice (and I hope ſufficiently) to prove, that the deſcent of the crown cannot *(de jure)* be impeach'd in the right line.

Having thus ſufficiently proved out of our books, that the power of the kings of England is an exempt, abſolute, ſupreme, and independent authority, acknowledging no ſuperior, but God Almighty, not to be divided, communicated nor transferred to any perſon whatſoever, without previous aſſent and conſent of the nation in parliament aſſembled. I proceed to ſhew the reader in the next place, that George the third, our now gracious ſovereign lord and king, is the lawful and undoubted heir of the blood royal of this realm, as appears by the pedigree following: and conſequently his moſt excellent majeſty, has the ſame abſolute, ſovereign and regal power over the ſubjects of this nation, that his royal predeceſſors, the kings and queens of England, have heretofore claimed and enjoyed.

## *The Royal Pedigree of* ENGLAND.

HENRY 7. by the father's ſide was the ſon of Edmond earl of Richmond, the grand-child of Owen, the ſon of Meredith Tudor, and Catherine the widow of H. 5. king of England, and daughter of Charles the ſixth king of France.

2. By the mother's ſide, he was the ſon of Margaret, grandſon of John Ghent duke of Lancaſter, great grandſon of Ed. 3. king of England.

### *Elizabeth.*

By the father's ſide. 1. By the father's ſide, was the daughter of Edward the fourth, king of England; grand-daughter of Richard, duke of York; great grand daughter of Richard of Cambridge; great, great grand-daughter of Edmund duke of York; the fifth ſon of Edward the third, king of England.

2. By

7. By the mother's ſide, ſhe was the daughter of Eliz. grand-daughter of Richard of Woodvill, earl of Rivers, and Jacoba dutcheſs of Bedford. By the mother's ſide.

By this H. 7. and his wife Elizabeth, were begotten.

1. Arthur, who died without iſſue.
2. Henry, who reigned after his father.
3. Edmund, who died in his infancy.
4. Margaret, who was married to James 4. king of Scots, who begat on her.

James 5. king of Scots.
Arthur,
Alexander,
and one Daughter.

This Margaret's ſecond huſband was Archibald Douglas, earl of Argyle, and ſhe had by him, Margaret who was married to Matthew duke of Lenox.

By this latter Margaret and Matthew, were born Henry, who died in his infancy; and Henry Darley, who married Mary queen of Scots; and by her begot James 6. of Scotland, and firſt of England, king; and Charles earl of Lenox, the father of Arabella.

5. Elizabeth, who died a child.

6. Mary, firſt the wife of Lewis the thirteenth king of France, by whom ſhe had no iſſue, and then ſhe was the wife of Charles Brandon duke of Suffolk; who had by her, Henry, Charles and Frances. This Frances was married to Henry Grey, marquiſs of Dorcheſter, and betwixt them was begat, Jane *regina infelix*.

7. Catherine, who died a child.

Henry the eighth, married firſt Catherine, the relict of his brother Arthur, and on her begat, Henry, who died in his youth; Mary, who afterwards reigned; Henry the eighth being devorced from this Catherine, married Ann of Bolen, by this queen, Henry the eighth had the lady Elizabeth, who afterwards reigned.

The ſecond wife being beheaded, Henry the eighth married Jane Seymour, by whom he had Edward the ſixth, who immediately after his father, reigned, and died without iſſue.

Mary

Mary was married to Philip king of Spain, and died without iſſue.

Elizabeth reigned, and was never married.

James 1. of England.

By the father's ſide, was the ſon of Henry Darley, grand-ſon of Mathew earl of Lenox, great grandſon of Archibald Douglas, and Margaret, the eldeſt daughter of H. 7.

By the mother's ſide, he was the ſon of Mary, queen of Scots, grand-ſon of James 5. king of Scotland, great grand-ſon of James 4. king of Scots, and Margaret, the firſt begotten daughter of Henry 7.

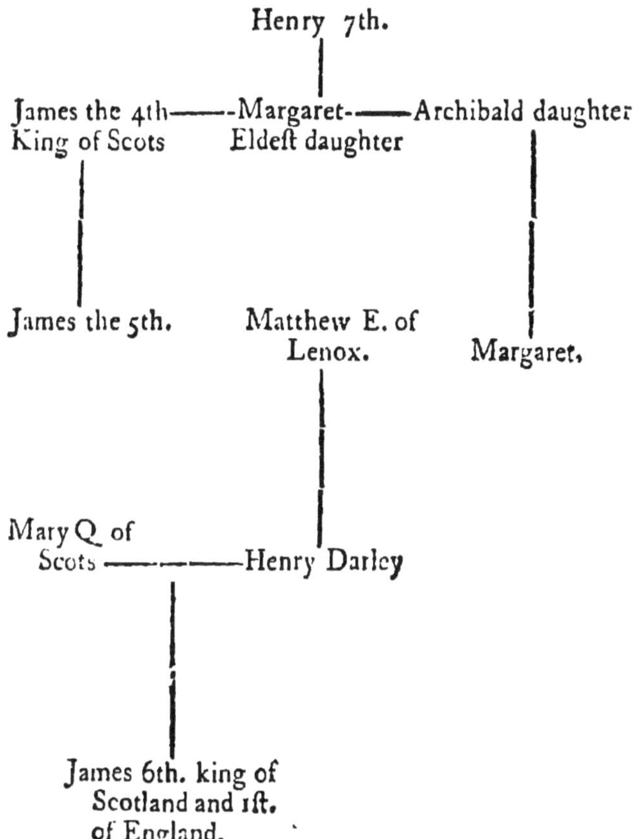


Upon the pedigree here set forth, was grounded the recognition of the lords and commons, in the first year of the said king. And it was, *That immediately upon the dissolution, and death of queen Elizabeth, the imperial crown of England, and of all the kingdoms belonging to the same, did by inherent birth-right, and lawful succession descend, and come to his most excellent majesty, as being lineally next, and sole heir to the blood royal of this realm.*

1 Jac. 6.

And it is worthy observation, that the whole right of the Saxons and Normans, and of the houses of York and Lancaster, were intirely united in king James.

This

This James, ſtiled king of Great-Britain, married Ann the daughter of Frederic 2. king of Denmark and Norway, by whom he had iſſue, two ſons and three daughters, *viz.*

1. Henry, who died in his father's life time, in the flower of his age, without iſſue.

2. Charles the firſt, (the royal martyr).

3. Elizabeth, who was married to Frederic V. elector palatine of the Rhine, and king of Bohemia; of this intermarriage was born the moſt excellent princeſs Sophia, who, in the year 1658, was married to Erneſt duke of Brunſwic Lunenburg, afterwards elector of Hanover, great, great grand-father of the illuſtrious Monarch, who now wears the imperial crown of Great-Britain.

4. Mary, who died young.

5. Sophia, who died in her infancy.

On the demiſe of James the firſt, Charles 1. his only ſurviving ſon, ſucceeded next. This unfortunate prince took to wiſe, the princeſs Henrietta Maria, daughter to the French king, Henry 4. and left behind him three ſons and three daughters, *viz.*

1. Charles, afterwards king of Great-Britain.

2. James, afterwards James the 2d. king of Great-Britain.

3. Henry, duke of Glouceſter, who died unmarried.

4. Mary, who married William prince of Orange, father to king William 3.

5. Elizabeth, who died a priſoner in the Iſle of Wight.

6. Henrietta, married to the duke of Orleans, only brother to Lewis the 14th.

Charles the ſecond, eldeſt ſon of Charles the firſt, ſucceeded his father, and on May the 8th. 1660, was proclaimed at London; he married Catherine of Portugal, but had no iſſue, he was therefore on his demiſe in 1684, ſucceeded by his brother the duke of York, by the name of James the 2d. who, while he was duke of York, had married Ann eldeſt daughter of Hyde, earl of Clarendon, by whom he had iſſue, the queens, Mary and Ann. By his ſecond conſort, an Italian princeſs, he had ſeveral, though ſhort-lived children, except another Mary, who was born, and died

died in France, aged twenty. But this James openly admitting father Petre, with ſeveral popiſh lords into his privy council, introducing popiſh judges into the courts of juſtice, and in direct violation of the coronation-oath, which he and his predeceſſors (from the reign of Henry 8. had now eſtabliſhed and confirmed into an indiſpenſable conſtitution of ſtate, the violation of which conſtitution, works of itſelf, an inability to reign over the proteſtant empire of Great-Britain, he, through a ſelf-evident conviction of ſuch inability, voluntarily abdicated the throne on the 11th. of December 1688, and as this realm admits of no *inter regnum*, the vacated crown, devolved on his elder daughter Mary, as the neareſt proteſtant heir, and *in her right* on her huſband William prince of Orange, by the names of

William 3. and Mary 2. but Mary dying in 1694, and William in 1701, without iſſue,

Ann, ſecond daughter of James 2. ſucceeded king William: this princeſs, for the ſecurity of the proteſtant religion in 1683, was married to his royal highneſs prince George of Denmark, and had iſſue, two ſons, and four daughters, who all died in their infancy.

Before I mention the kings of the houſe of Hanover, it will be proper to ſhew the ſeveral branches of the blood royal of England, and the ſettlement of the crown in the Proteſtant Line.

There are two branches of the preſent royal family; the one Proteſtant, and the other Popiſh; the latter is nearer in deſcent, but the former inherits the crown by the laws of the realm.

Henrietta, the youngeſt daughter of Charles 1. was married to Philip duke of Orleans, only brother to Lewis 14. by whom ſhe had two daughters, the younger of which was married to Victor 2. duke of Savoy. Their iſſue were Charles 1. king of Sardinia, and two daughters: the elder married the late duke of Burgundy Dauphin, father of the French king Lewis 15. the other married Philip 5. king of Spain.

The palatine branch contains a numerous iſſue. The root is the lady Elizabeth, daughter of king James 1. who married Frederic 5. elector palatine of the Rhine. In 1619, he was crowned king of Bohemia, but loſt both that kingdom and the palatinate upon the defeat of his forces near Prague, by Ferdinand the emperor; and died at Mentz, 1632. The princess Elizabeth, his queen dowager, died at Craven-house in Drury-lane, London, 1661.

By the said princess he had six sons, Charles, Rupert, Maurice, Edward, Philip, Gustavus; and four daughters, of which Sophia only had children. And of the sons, Charles and Edward only had issue.

Charles succeeded his father in the palatinate, by the treaty of Munster, and left one son and a daughter by Charlotte his wife, of Hesse-Cassel. Rupert and Maurice, both died batchelors; the first in England: Edward lived in France, where he turned papist, and married Ann of Mantua, from which match came a numerous offspring.

The son of Charles succeeded also by that name in the Palatinate; but dying without issue, the Palatinate fell to the popish family of Neuburg.

Elizabeth, daughter of the elector Charles, was the second wife of Philip, duke of Orleans, who had by her the duke of Orleans, regent of France; and Elizabeth married to Leopold duke of Lorrain, who was father to Francis and Charles of Lorrain; Francis married the queen of Hungary, Charles married her sister.

Edward, the youngest son of the unfortunate king of Bohemia, married, as I said before, Ann of Mantua, by whom he had three daughters, Ann, Benedict, and Lucy, which last never married.

Ann married the prince of Condé, of the house of Bourbon; Benedicta married John duke of Hanover; by whom he had two daughters: Charlotte, the first, married the duke of Modena; and Wilhelmina married the emperor Joseph.

I conclude with the protestant branch of the royal family, in the house of Hanover, which begins with the princess Sophia, sister to Charles and Edward aforesaid, whose offspring we have seen.

This most excellent princess, the fourth and youngest daughter of Frederick 4, elector Palatine of the Rhine, and king of Bohemia, and of Elizabeth of Great-Britain, was in the year 1658, married to Ernest duke of Brunswick and Lunenburg, afterwards elector of Hanover; which duke Ernest succeeded to the bishoprick of Osnabrug; and also to the dukedom of Hanover, upon the death of his elder brother John, who died without male issue, 1680.

The elector Ernest had issue by the said Sophia, George, afterwards king of Great-Britain; Frederic slain in Transilvania 1690, valiantly fighting against the Turks; Maximilian, the third son, deceased; Charles, the fourth son, slain at the battle of Cassaneck in Albania, 1690. Christian, fifth son, shot in the river Danube, crossing to charge the French, at the battle of Munderkingen, in 1703. Ernest duke of York and bishop of Osnaburg: Sophia, their only daughter, was married to Frederick, the first king of Prussia, who married with his cousin-german, Sophia Dorothy, only daughter of king George 1. and had Charles king of Prussia, and a numerous issue.

Pursuant to the act of settlement on the death of queen Ann, the princess Sophia also dying two months before; George the next indisputable protestant heir, was on the 1st. of August, 1714, being Sunday, proclaimed king of Great-Britain, *&c.* by the unanimous voice of the people.

But George the 1st. demising in 1727, left issue by his royal consort the lady Sophia, daughter of his uncle the duke of Zell, one only daughter named Sophia, married to Frederick 2. king of Prussia, and one only son, George prince of Wales, who immediately succeeded by the name of George 2. who, by his consort Caroline princess royal of Prussia, had issue two sons and four daughters, *viz.*

1. Frederick, prince of Wales, married to the most excellent princess Augusta, sister to Frederic 3. duke of Saxe-Gotha.

2. William, duke of Cumberland.

3. Ann, married to the late prince of Orange and Nassau.

4. Amelia Sophia, unmarried.

5. Mary, married to William, now landgrave of Hesse Cassel.

6. Louisa, late consort to Frederic 5. king of Denmark.

Frederick, by his consort, her royal highness the princess of Wales now living, had issue five sons, and four daughters, namely.

 1. George,

1. George, our present illustrious monarch.

2. Edward Augustus, now duke of York and Albany.

3. William Henty,

4. Henry Frederic.

5. Frederic William.

6. Augusta, now bethrothed to the hereditary prince of Brunswick-Wolfembuttle.

7. Elizabeth Caroline, deceased.

8. Louisa Ann.

9. Caroline Matilda.

His royal highness Frederick prince of Wales, deceasing in 1751, and George the second in 1759, the imperial crown of Great-Britain, devolved on his eldest grand-son, George the third, our present, incomparable Sovereign.

I shall add one word with respect to the pre-eminence of our kings, a pre-eminence superior to that either of France or Spain, as appears in a debate of this kind boldly ascertained, and peremptorily insisted upon by our English orators in the council of Constance, Anno 1417,(a) when it was urged and alledged by them, as an argument in the contest between our Henry the fifth's legates, and those of Charles the sixth, the then French king, for *precedence*; "*satis constat*, (say they) (b) *secundum Albertum magnum et Bartholemeum de proprietatibus rerum, quod toto mundo in tres partes diviso, scilicet in Europam, asciamet Africam* (for America was not then discovered) *Europa in quatuor dividitur regna scilicit primum Romanum, secundum Constantinopolitanum, tertium regnum* HIBERNIÆ *(quod jam translatum est in Anglos) et quartun regnum Hispaniæ. Ex quo patet, quod rex Angliæ et regnum suum sunt de eminentioribus et antiquioribus regibus et regnis* TOTIUS *Europæ.*" And accordingly the antiquity and precedence was then allowed him, wholly on the account of his kingdom of Ireland. And agreeable to this right of precedence, Pope Urban the second, caused the archbishop of Canterbury, when in the council of Cleremont, to sit at his feet, and DECREED that he should take the same place in all future councils, *tanquam alterius orbis pontificem*", and as a farther proof, it is on record, that upon the division of Christianity into nations, at the two general councils of Constance and Pisa, (the first, by

(a) Selden's Tit. hors. par. 1. c. 8. sect. 5. Usher, archbishop of Armagh, of the religion of the ancient Irish cap. 11.

(b) Act. Council. Constant. ses. 28. M. S. in Bib. Reg. not in the printed acts.

by much the greateſt that ever was held, the laſt, not the leaſt) England gave voice as one fourth part of Chriſtendom, the other three parts were France, Germany, and Italy, which being Iberia Major, contained Spain, as Iberia Major.

Now George 3d. wearing the imperial crown of Great-Britain, France and Ireland, with other and much more extenſive dominions dependant on the Britiſh diadem, and being our undoubted and lawful liege lord, according to the forementioned pedigreee, may challenge (amongſt others) theſe prerogatives following, as incident to the imperial crown of Great-Britain, ſome of which are the very eſſence of ſovereign power, and ſome of them annext to the regality by the municipal laws, and old cuſtoms of the lands.

---

## 1. Prerogative.

*His Majeſty as to the coercive part of the law, is ſubject to none under God.*

GOD intending the good of mankind, which is not to be obtained without preſervation of order; hath commanded us to be ſubject to the ſupreme authority; not to offer any manner of violence to the perſon of him, in whom is veſted ſovereign majeſty. The ſanctitude of whoſe perſon is ſo great, that we are not to ſpeak evil of it, no, not to think, much leſs to hazard the power, or injure the perſon, either by force or judicial proceedings. Liber ab omni legum Coactione.

The authorities that I intend for the proof of this prerogative are theſe:

Bracton and Fleta, ſay thus: If any thing be demanded of the king by a ſubject, (ſeeing a writ lieth not againſt him) he is put to his petition, praying to correct and amend his own fact; which, if he will not, it is a ſufficient penalty for him, that he is to expect a puniſhment from the Lord. No man may preſume to diſpute of what the king does, much leſs to reſiſt him. Bract. lib. 1. c. 8. lib. 5. c. 3. de defaltis Fleta lib. 2. c. 17.

Sir John Markham, chief juſtice, told king Ed. 4. that the king cannot arreſt any man for ſuſpicion of 1. H. 7. 4. b.

treaſon

treaſon or felony, as other of his lieges may: for that if it be a wrong to the party grieved, the ſubject has no remedy.

3 Ed. 3. 19. Co. 4. Inſt. 17. Co. lib. 1. 44. b. Plowd. Com. 24. Co. Lit. 19. b.

The king has no peer in his land, and therefore cannot be judged.

Our law ſays, that the king can do no wrong, and therefore cannot be puniſhed; and the reaſon why it is ſaid in our law, that the king cannot do a tort, is, becauſe nothing can be done in this realm by any act of the king, as to the ſubject's lands or liberties, but muſt be approved by the eſtabliſhed laws of this realm, which the judges are ſworn to obſerve and deliver, between the king and his ſubjects; and therefore the judges and miniſters of juſtice, are to be queſtioned and puniſhed if the laws be violated, and no reflection to be made on the king. *Si factum injuſtum fuerit* (ſays Bracton) *perinde non erit factum regis.*

Co. lib. 7. Calvin's caſe.

The Spencers in Ed. 2. Time, hatcht to cover their treaſon, this moſt horrid opinion, *viz.*

That homage and the oath of allegiance, was more by reaſon of the king's crown, (that is of his politic capacity) than by reaſon of the perſon of the king, uppon which opinion, they inferred theſe curſed principles:

1. If the king demeaned himſelf not according to reaſon in the right of the crown, his lieges are bound by oath to remove him.

2. Seeing the king could not be removed by ſuit of law, it was to be done by force.

3. That the ſubjects be obliged to govern in default of him.

All which moſt abominable tenets were condemned by two parliaments, one in the reign of Ed. 2. called *Exilium Hugonis le Spencer*, and the other in the reign of Ed. 3. And the ſeparation of the king's perſon from his power, is the principal article condemned.

12. Carol. 2 Regis c. 30. The attainder of ſeveral perſons guilty of the horrid

To conclude, it was declared by the lords and commons in parliament, *That by the undoubted and fundamental laws of the kingdom, neither the peers of this realm, nor the commons, nor both together in parliament, nor the people collectively, nor repreſentatively, nor any other perſons whatſoever, ever had, hath, or ought to have any coercive power over the perſons of the kings of England.*

With

With our laws do concur the laws imperial, *Sacrilegii instar est rescripto principis obviare: unde ipse legibus civilibus non astringitur. Nam in omnibus imperatoris excipitur fortuna cui ipsas leges Deus subjecit.*

murder of king Cha. I.

Zoucheus pars 4. sect. 4. de jure principis.

*Princeps legibus solutus est*, says *Justinian*; That is to say, the power of all monarchs, is *legibus soluta*, subject to no over-ruling power of man. Conceive it not so, that kings are free from the direction of, and obligation to the law of God, nature, and common equity; but from the coercion human, or any human coactive power, to punish, censure or dethrone them.

More of this excellent learning the reader may see in doctor Duck, *lib.* 1. *c.* 3. *num.* 1 & 2. *de authoritate juris civilis.* Sir Walter Raleigh, *hist. pars* 1. *lib.* 2. *c.* 4. *sect.* 16. Mr. Rober Coke, *lib.* 2. *c.* 3. *num.* 5, 6.

---

## 2. Prerogative.

### *Power of making Laws.*

Legem ferendarum summa potestas.

THE king in a double respect is the life of our laws, he is the life of our peace, without which our laws are put to silence; and again, because laws are *literæ mcutuæ* without the stamp of his royal authority: and therefore the agreeing votes of the two houses of parliament are not conclusive to his majesty's judgment, nor can they carry with them his royal assent, whom they do not represent in any kind; nor is the king any further obliged to concur with the votes of the lords and commons, than he sees them conformable to the laws of God and nature, agreeable with his sacred rights and prerogatives as a sovereign, and tending to the general good and welfare of his loving subject:

In proof of this position, these authorities may be offered.

Though a bill hath passed both houses of the lords and commons in parliament, yet before it be a law, the royal assent must be asked or demanded, and obtained.

It is no ſtatute if the king's royal ſanction be not to it, and he may diſaſſent; for the king in parliament hath a negative voice, and therefore in a clauſe made 2 H. 5. both houſes of parliament do acknowledge that it is of the kings regality, to grant or deny ſuch of their petitions as pleaſeth himſelf.

13. Car. 2. Regis c. 1. It is declared, that there can be no legiſlative power in either or both houſes of parliament without the king.

But upon what hath been ſaid, it may be objected, that ſeeing his majeſty cannot enact laws without the lords and commons, (for every ſtatute, as appears in our books muſt be made by the king, with the aſſent of the lords and commons) the legiſlative power is not ſolely in the king, but in him and the two houſes of parliament; ſo that they fancy the two houſes partners of the ſovereignty, and turn the monarchy of England, into a tripartite and co-ordinate government, which others call a mixt monarchy.

4. H. 7. 18. b. Co. Lit. 159. 6. Co. 4. Inſt. 25.

I anſwer, that to the two houſes of parliament, belongs a right of privilege, for the making of laws, by yielding their conſent; but that they have a co-ordinate, co-equal, corrival and collateral power with the ſovereignty of royalty, all able juriſts, and true politicians utterly deny; for the houſes are called together by the royal authority, not to be dictators but Councellors; not to be Partners in the Legiſlature, but Petitioners? as appears by the very form of paſſing bills at this very day obſerved, *Le Roy le veult & fait come ill eſt deſirè*, which form of words ſhew, that the rogation of laws, belongeth to the two houſes, but the Legiſlation to the king, it is the king's great *prerogative* to be thus *pre-roged*; their act, that is to ſay, the act of the two houſes is the Preparative, his only Juſſive; or if you will, though the king doth not *abſolutè ſolus*, yet *principaliter ſolus*, he maketh laws concerning matters eccleſiaſtical, capital, civil, martial, maritime, and the like.

But yet farther; if the two houſes of parliament do retain their proportion in the legiſlation, that is to ſay, if they have a co-ordinate or concurring power, with the king in enacting laws; then they muſt have it, either Originally in themſelves, or from ſome other quarter, by way of Derivation.

First,

First, they cannot have this coordination of power, originally and radically vested in themselves; for (as to the lords) Mr. Bracton tells us, that the earls and barons, were not before the first king; for says he, *Reges associant sibi Comites, & Barones, ordinantes eos, in magno Honore:* earls and barons are made by the king, and assumed for counsel, therefore invested with a long robe; and for defence, therefore girt with a sword; which shews, the power they have is not originally in themselves, but proceeds from the kings grant and favour; they are meer concessions of grace.

Dodridges tract of the nobility, pag. 8. 34. Co. lib 7. Nevils Case Co. 2. Inst 5, 6. lib. 12. earl of Shrewsbury's case.

As for the house of commons, I hope they will not pretend to any ancient or better title than the lords can pretend to. Sure it is (says sir Robert Filmer) that during the heptarchy, the people did not elect any knights, because England was not then divided into shires or counties.

All our books can inform us, that the king is *Principium, Caput, & finis Parliamenti,* and that every member, as well as both houses, have their right, and sitting there from him; they are summoned to sit in that council, by virtue of the kings writ and authority, without whose call they cannot meet together, and at whose pleasure they are dissolved in law and bound to depart to their own homes.

Secondly, as the two houses have not a Partnership in the supremacy, or Legislation originally in themselves, so neither have they it, by way of derivation; if the houses have a coordinate, coequal, and corival authority in enacting laws, derivately, then it must proceed from the king, one of these two ways, that is to say, either by way of grant, or by way of custom and prescription.

1. They cannot have it, *via Concessionis,* by way of grant; for kings reign by a higher than any human law, and therefore no act of any king can divest himself or successor of any essential attribute of power due to him or to his successor. And if kings actions did oblige themselves or successors, then were this crown not free, but subject to the pope, because our king John made it so; but I do utterly deny, that ever any king of this realm did ever grant the parliament or either house, a concurring power or fellowship of making laws with him;

Vide treatise intituled Sacro-SanctaRegum Majestati.

tis true they have an indefeisable right *ad aliquid*, to some act, of exercising the supreme power; that is to say, to the making of laws, by giving their assent, without which no statute is binding. Co. 4. Inst. 25. Co. Litt. 159. b.

And this right belongs to the houses, by a fundamental constitution of the kingdom; a fundamental I say, not of monarchy simply, but of government as it now stands; a fundamental not of the regal power, but of the people's security: for government may receive a change and qualification, by consent of king and people, from more absolute, to qualified, or restrained, and such a constitution is a fundamental, because all after-laws are built upon it, but not a fundamental to the regal power, for it gives no new power to the king, as it does to the two houses, but rather lessens his power, by limiting upon agreement, that he will not impose any laws upon his people without their consent.

2. They cannot have it *via præscriptionis*, by way of prescription; for no usage, prescription or custom can take place, where there are records or proofs enough to the contrary; and whether there are not proofs to the contrary, let the reader take so much pains as to view the styles of the acts printed from 9. H. 3. untill H. 7. his time, and he will find, that the king always made the law, and the lords spiritual and temporal did assent, at the instance, request, or petition of the commons, or by the king, with the assent of the lords and commons, which was not or but rarely used, unless in Richard the second's time. In Henry the seventh's time, the commons got to have their assent as well as the lords in passing laws; and this manner of passing laws continued generally untill Edward the sixth's time, when they were made sometime by the king, with the assent of the lords spiritual and temporal and commons in parliament, and sometimes by the parliament. But the form of enacting laws by the king and the lords spiritual, temporal, and commons assembled in parliament was seldom or ever used before queen Mary's time.

Vide Mr. Roger Coke lib. 3. c. 3. of the municipal laws of England, f. 115. 116.

So that we may very well conclude, by what has been said against coordination, *That the making of laws is a peculiar and incommunicable privilege of the supreme power; and that the office of the two houses in this case is only*

*only consultive or preparative, but the character of the power rests in the final sanction, which is in the king*; and therefore when the lords and commons present any bill to the king, and he passes it; this is an act of parliament, which is no more a law of the lords and commons, than the laws passed at the petition or rogation of Celius, Cassius, Sempronius &c. were the laws of Celius, Cassius, and Sempronius.

Let the reader note this maxim for a conclusion, viz, though the king cannot make new, or abrogate old laws, without consent in parliament; yet the interpretation of these Laws solely belongs to his majesty; for Mr. Bracton in the reign of H. 3. tells us, that in doubtful and obscure points, the interpretation and will of the king, is to be expected, *Since it is his part to interpret, who made the law.* In a word, our king hath as much right by our constitutions as that civil law gave the Roman emperor; *Inter equitatem Jusque inter positam Interpretationem nobis solis & licet, & oportet inspicere. L.* 1. *c. de Leg. & Constit.* or that other; *Rex solus judicat de Causa â Jure non definita.*

---

## 3. Prerogative.

### *Power of calling and assembling Parliaments.*

THE king is armed with divers councils, of which the court of parliament is the highest and most transcendent, consisting of the kings most excellent majesty, sitting there as supreme head, in his royal politick capacity, and of (*a*) three estates, the lords

Jus convocandorum comitiorum.

(*a*) for in our laws, the clergy, nobility, and commonalty are three estates. We your said most loving, &c. Subjects, viz. The lords spiritual and temporal, and the commons, representing your three estates of your realm of England. 1 Eliz. c. 3. The clergy being one of the greatest states of this realm. 8 Eliz. c. 1. This court consisteth (says Coke in 4. Inst. f. 1.) of the king, &c. and of the three estates of the realm. Of the lords spiritual and temporal, and commons.

spiritual, the lords temporal, and the commons of the realm, the calling and assembling of which three estates, is a part of the supreme power or regal prerogative, inseparably annext to the sacred person of the king; on whose royal pleasure, as the convoking, so the appointment of time and place for the holding of parliaments, their prorogation, adjournment, continuation, dissolution, do solely depend.

The authorities intended for the proof of this prerogative, are these:

Co. Lit. 110. a Co. 4. Inst. f. 6. &. 28.

None can begin (says Coke) continue, or dissolve the parliament, but by the king's authority.

16 Car. 1. c. 1.

In the reign of king Charles the first, it was declared, that the appointment of time and place for the holding of parliaments, hath always belonged, as it ought, to his majesty and his royal progenitors.

16 Car. 2. Regis.

In the reign of Charles 2. It is acknowledged, that it is a prerogative inherent to the imperial crown of England, the calling and assembling of parliaments.

Co. 4. Inst f. 46. Rot Parl. 1 H. 5. num. 26.

Note, as all commissions concerning the administration of justice, do determine by the demise of the king, so upon his decease, a parliament then in being, is absolutely dissolved; yea, though an act of parliament be made, that the parliament shall not be dissolved, but by act of parliament, as the statute 16, 17 Car. 1. c. 7. Which parliament is declared to be dissolved upon the death of the royal martyr. Vide 12 Car. 2. c. 1. and 13 Car. 2. c. 1. By 6. Ann. c. 7. it is declared that the parliament shall not be dissolved by the death of her majesty, or her successor; nor the privy council, officers civil and military &c. discharged, but to act and continue in their offices for six months, unless prorogued or discarded by the successor. So that this act still leaves the royal prerogative in its full force, by not presuming absolutely to determine all offices on the demise of the sovereign, but leaving the sovereign next in succession the option whether he will determine them or not.

## 4. Prerogative.

### *Power of life and Death.*

JUSTICE and mercy (the brightest stars in the sphere of majesty) are incidents inseparable to an imperial throne. The exercising the sword, as well as of calling parliaments; of punishing, rewarding, and pardoning, as well as reigning, is a prerogative inherent to the crown of England. Potestas vitæ ac necis.

The authorities for the proof of this prerogative are these.

*Rex* (says our *Bracton*) *potestatem habet judicandi, de Vita, & Membris, vel tollendi Vitam, vel concedendi.* Lib. 3. c. 8. de Corona.

*Vita & Membra hominum ad tuitionem, vel ad pœnam cum deliquerint, in potestate Regum sunt.* Fleta lib. c. 16.

*A Chescun Roy, per reason de son office, il appent a fair justice en execution des Leyes, Grace, en granter pardons*, &c. 9 Ed. 4. 2. a.

*Jam si quispiam rei capitalis, reus proposcerit regis misericordiam pro foris facto suo timidus mortis, vel membrorum perdendorum potest ei lege suæ dignitatis condonare, si velit etiam mortem promeritam.* Inter leges Edvardi Lambard. fol. 143.

But it is to be understood, as indeed the statue of 2 E. 3. c. 2, explains it, that no charter for murder, &c. is to be granted, but where one killeth another in his own defence, or by misadventure: and by the stat. of 14 E. 3. c. 15. it is further explained and promulgated, "that no pardon of the death of any man to be granted, or other felony, but where the king may do it, consistent with his coronation oath; and by 16 R. 2. c. 9. the king thought proper to notify and declare, that where the offence is found wilful murder, no pardon is to be allowed, and in appeal of death the king will not pardon."

By the statute of 27 H. 8. c. 24. It is declared, that no man can pardon treasons, murders, man-slaughters, or any kind of felonies, but the king only.

With our law doth concur the civil law, *ad majestatem spectat potestas vitæ ac necis, cum solus princeps primario habeat jus gladii; unde pœna minui, & restitutio in integrum concedi duntaxat a principe potest.* Zo pars 4. sect. 4. de jure principis.

5. Pre-

## 5. Prerogative.

### *Power of restoring infamous persons to their former Credits.*

Jus infames famæ restituendi.

ALthough the poet tells us, *pœna potest redimi, culpa perennis erit*, pardon may discharge a man of punishment, but the scandal of the offence remains; yet in our law, when the king doth grant a pardon to any subject, for an offence perpetrated against the dignity of the crown; the king by that pardon, doth not only take away the punishment, but likewise cleareth the person of the crime and infamy in which no private man is interested, but the common-wealth, of which the king is the head, and in whom all general injuries reside, and to whom the reformation of all public wrongs doth appertain; and therefore, a man can no more call another thief or traitor, after a general or special pardon, than to say, a man is a villain, that is manumized.

In proof of this prerogative, this authority may be produced.

Hobart's Reports, Cuddington v. Wilkins f. 67, 81, 294.

An action of the case was brought, for calling a man thief; the defendant justified, alledging, that the plaintiff had stolen somewhat: the plaintiff replied, that since the supposed felony, the general pardon in the 7th. year of the king was made, and makes the usual averment to bring himself within the pardon; upon which averment the defendant demurred, and it was adjudged for the plaintiff: for the whole court were of opinion, that though he were a thief once, yet when the pardon came, it took away not only *pœnam* but *reatum:* for felony is *contra coronam & dignitatem regis*.

To shew further, the force of the king's pardon, I will subjoin this case, *viz.*

2 Ed. 3. Cor. 134. Co. 3 inst. fol. 237.

If in an appeal of felony, the defendant doth offer trial by battle; the plantiff may counter-plead it, by saying, that the defendant being apprehended, escaped or brake prison, which presumes a guiltiness: now, if the king pardon the breaking of prison, the counter-plea fails, and the defendant shall be restored to the battle: and yet the reason of the presumption

ſumption of the guiltineſs is the ſame after the pardon, as it was before. But the reaſon of the caſe is, that the king's pardon doth not only clear the offence itſelf, but all the dependencies, penalties and diſabilities incident unto it, and that againſt the appellant.

That his majeſty hath power not only to confer grace, but alſo to deliver ſubjects from the reproach of their former miſcarriages: let the reader look into the ſtatutes of 12 Car. 2. c. 11. 13 Car. 2. c. 1.

---

## 6. Prerogative.

### *Power of creating Magiſtrates.*

ANnexed to the ſovereignty of England, is the right of judicature, of hearing and deciding all controverſies; for this kingdom (as all other kingdoms in their conſtitution) is with the power of juſtice, according to the rules of law and equity, both which being in the king as ſovereign, were ſettled in ſeveral courts, as the light being firſt made by God, was after placed in the great bodies of the ſun and moon; and therefore the lord chancellor, (or lord keeper) the judges of the realm, and all other juſtitiaries, are but miniſters to his majeſty, who (being not able alone to manage all matters and proceedings in law) hath delegated the power of juſtice to theſe perſons to be his inſtruments; by which delegation his majeſty's power is conveyed to every place, where the virtue of it is extended.

Poteſtas conſtituendorum magiſtratuum ad juſtitiam expediendam.

The authorities to be produced in proof of this prerogative, are theſe:

I will begin with Bracton, (a man worthily famous for his knowledge, in the civil and common law).

*Sciendum*, ſays he, *quod ipſe Dominus Rex, qui ordinariam habet juriſdictionem, & dignitatem, & poteſtatem ſuper omnes, qui in regno ſuo ſunt: habet enim omnia jura in manu ſuâ, quæ ad coronam & laicalem pertinent poteſtatem, & materialem gladium, qui pertinet ad regni gubernaculum:*

Lib. 2. c. 24.

*naculum: habet etiam justitiam, & judicium, quæ sunt jurisdictiones, ut ex jurisdictione suâ, sic ut Dei minister, & vicarius, tribuat unicuique quod suum fuerit: habet etiam coercionem, ut delinquentes puniat, et coerceat. Item habet in potestate sua leges & constitutiones, assisas in regno suo provisas, &c. ipse in propriâ personâ suâ observet, & subditis suis faciat observari, nihil enim prodest jura condere, nisi sit qui jura tueatur.* The English of it is this; the king hath supreme power in all civil causes, and is over all persons; all jurisdictions are in him; the material sword of right belongs to him, and whatsoever conduces to peace, that the people committed to his charge may lead peaceable and quiet lives. The power of holding assizes is derived from him, and of punishing delinquents; for laws were vainly enacted if there were not some person enabled to protect us by defending them, *&c.*

The author of the book called the Mirror, expresses himself thus: *Judgment vient de jurisdiction que est la*
Cap. 4. 4 *pluis grand dignity quæ appert al Roy. Jurisdiction ne*
sect. 2. &. *peut nul assigner forsque le Roy. Le Roy per le authoritie*
sect. 4. *de sa dignitie fait justices en divers degrees, & limit a chescun poiar.*

King E. 1. in the beginning of his book of laws, called Breton, declares, *that he is God's vicegerent, & that he hath distributed his charge into several portions,* confessing himself not able alone to hear and determine all the complaints of his subjects.

Lib.1.c.17 *Non potest aliquis* (says Fleta) *judicare in temporalibus nisi solus rex, vel subdelegatus*

12 H. 7. 17. b. *All commencement, tout L' administration de justice fut en une main,* viz. *en le corone, donques, apres multiplication de peuple, administration de justice fut devide,* &c.

Co.lib.12. case of conspiracy, f. 25. The king himself is *de jure* to deliver justice to all his subjects, and because he himself cannot do it to all persons, he delegates his power to his judges, who have the custody, and guard of the king's oath.

Brad. against Atw. p. 28, and 46. It is enacted by 27 H. 8. c. 24. That no person of whatsoever condition, shall have any power to make any justices of the peace, or justices of goal-delivery; but all such officers shall be made by letters patent, under the great seal, in the name and authority of the king and his heirs, in all shires, counties, counties palatine,

palatine, and other places of the realm. This act is a recontinuance of liberties taken from the crown.

*Sine warranto juriſdictionem nemo habet*, ſaith Bracton; nor can any one appoint a ſubſtitute under him, but every judge is bound to officiate *propriâ perſonâ*, the juſtice in eyre only excepted, and that by a particular ſtatute for particular reaſons there expreſſed.

With our laws agrees the law imperial, *ad curam principis magiſtratuum creatio pertinet non ad populi favorem in L. un. ff. ad legem amb.*

*Creatio magiſtratuum* (ſays Zonarius) *maxima pars eſt imperatorii muneris.*

---

## 7. Prerogative.

### *Power of making War, and the ſole diſpoſition of the Militia.*

IT is the office of the king to defend, and by arms to protect his people; and the power of war, as the power of the ſword, is a branch of his imperial authority; and that no way impartible to any perſon but either to the king himſelf, in whom reſides the ſupreme power, or to thoſe that are commiſſionated by him. Jus belli ſuſcipiendi.

Authorities in proof of this prerogative are theſe:

Wars make aliens enemies, and *bellum indicere* belongeth only to the king. Co. lib. 7. Calvin's caſe.

No ſubject can levy war within the realm, without authority from the king, for to him only it appertaineth. Co. 3. Inſt, f 9. F. N. b. f. 113. a.

The prelates, earls, barons, and commonalty of this realm declared, *That to the king it belongeth, and his part it is, through his royal ſigniory ſtraitly to defend by force of arms, and all other force againſt his peace at all times, when it ſhall pleaſe him, and to puniſh them which ſhall do contrary, according to the laws, and uſages of this his realm.* Co. lib. 9. Wiſeman's caſe. An. 7. E. 1.

And accordingly in parliament, in after times, the king alone did iſſue his proclamations, to prohibit



bearing

bearing of arms by any perſon, in or near the city, where the parliament was, excepting ſuch of the king's ſervants, as he ſhould depute, or ſhould be deputed by his commandment, and alſo excepting the king's miniſters.

And this power of raiſing forces to be ſolely in the king, is ſo known, and inſeparable a right to the imperial diadem; that when in the reign of H. 8. there being a ſudden rebellion, the earl of Shrewſbury, without warrant from the king, did raiſe armies for the ſuppreſſion of it, and happily ſuppreſſed it; yet was he forced to obtain the royal pardon.

If any levy war to expulſe ſtrangers, to deliver men out of priſons, to remove counſellors, or againſt any ſtatute, or to any other end, pretending reformation of their own heads, without warrant from the king, this is levying a war againſt the king, becauſe they take upon them royal authority, which is againſt the king.

Co. 3. Inſt. 160. 11. H. 7. 22. If any perſon by mutual aſſent, do uſe juſts, or turnaments, or play at ſword and buckler, or any other deeds of arms, and the one killeth the other, this is felony, becauſe it is not lawful to uſe them without the king's licence.

Britan. c. 20. Co. Litt. 5. a. Co. 2. Inſt. 30. Co. 3. Juſt. 201. No ſubject can build a caſtle or houſe of ſtrength imbattelled, or other fortreſs defenſible, without licenſe from the king. Although theſe authorities aforeſaid are ſufficient to demonſtrate to the reader, that by the laws of the land, the power of raiſing forces or armies, or levying war, for the defence of the kingdom, or otherwiſe, hath always belonged to the king, and to him only; yet I will add one authentique evidence more, and it ſhall be the ſtatute of 13 Car. 2. c. 6. which is not a conſtitutive law, but an act declarative, not introductory of a new law, but declaratory of the old fundamental laws of this realm in this point of prerogative.

13 Car. 2. c. 6 vide 14 Car. 2. c. 3. In the reign of Charles 2. it was declared, that within his majeſty's realms and dominions, the ſupreme government, command and diſpoſition of the militia, and of all the forces by ſea and land, and all forts and places of ſtrength is, and by the laws of England, ever was the undoubted right of his majeſty, and his royal

royal predeceſſors, kings and queens of England, and that both or either of the houſes of parliament, cannot or ought to pretend to the ſame, nor can, nor lawfully may raiſe or levy any war offenſive or defenſive, againſt his majeſty, his heirs, or lawful ſucceſſors.

Note, that the kings of this realm ſtill uſed to refer cauſes petitioned in parliament, to the proper places of cognizance and deciſion; but for matter of war and peace, the kings ever kept it in *ſcrinio pectoris*, in the ſhrines of their own breaſts, aſſiſted and adviſed by their council of ſtate. As for example:

In the 4th year of Ed. 3. the commons petitioned, that the king would enter into certain covenants and capitulations with the duke of Brabant; in which petition, there was alſo inſerted ſomewhat touching a money-matter; the king's anſwer was, that for what concerned the monies, they might handle it, and examine it; but touching the peace, he would do as to himſelf ſeemed good.

In the ſecond year of K. R. 2. the merchants of the ſea-coaſts, did complain of divers ſpoils upon their ſhips and goods by the Spaniards. The king's anſwer was, that with the advice of his council, he would procure remedy.

In 50 Ed. 3. The merchants of York petitioned in Parliament againſt the Hollanders; and deſired the Dutch ſhips might be ſtayed both in England and at Calais. The king's anſwer was, let it be declared to the king's council, and they ſhall have ſuch remedy, as is according to reaſon. I will add one more, and that is a very remarkable precedent; and it is in 17 R. 2. This king made offer to the commons in Parliament, that they ſhould take into their conſiderations matters of war and peace then in hand. The commons in modeſty excuſed themſelves, and anſwered: *the commons will not preſume to treat of ſo high a charge.* The reader may ſee more of theſe matters in ſir Francis Bacon's Reports in the houſe of commons, of ſpeeches delivered by the earls of Saliſbury, and of Northampton, and at a conference, touching the petition of merchants. Parl. 5. Jacob.

Agreeable to our laws is that which the doctors of the imperial law aſſert, viz. *In communione militari primus eſt, & ſupremam poteſtatem obtinet imperator*;

 nam

*nam post quam lege regia, populus in imperatorem omnem suam potestatem contulit, ad ipsum etiam belli & pacis arbitrium devolutum est.*

In the Codes of Justinian, is extant the constitution of the emperor's *Valentinian & Valens*; *nulli prorsus nobis insciis, atque inconsultis, quorum libet armorum movendorum copia tribuatur.* Agreeable to which is that of St. Austin: *Ordo naturalis mortalium paci accomodatus hoc poscit; ut suscipiendi belli authoritas atque consilium penes principes sit.*

---

## 8. Prerogative.

### *Power of making leagues and truces with foreign Princes.*

Fœderum percussio penes regem.

AS it appertaineth to his majesty, to provide that peace be continued in the heart of his empire; and that things contrary to public quiet be by foresight prevented and avoided; so it is inherent to his royal dignity, to procure amity, to make leagues and truces with foreign states, and to maintain them, by preventing whatsoever may tend to the violation of truce and safe conduct.

The authorities for proof of this prerogative are these:

Co. lib. 7. Calvin's case.

Leagues between our sovereign and others, are the only means to make aliens friends; *& fœdera percutere*, to makes leagues, only and wholly pertaineth to the king.

2H.5.c.6.

To the king only it belongs to make leagues with foreign princes.

19 E.4.6. Co.4.Inst. f. 152.

Brian held, that if *all* the subjects of England would make war with any king in league with the king of England, without the assent of the king of England, that such a war was no breach of the league.

All addresses of state are made to our kings without any obligation to bind the crown to communicate any thing to any of the members of the great council, privy council, or common council, much less to either of the ministers

ministers of state, whether secretaries or not, however sworn to secrecy and trust. Nor requires there a more pregnant instance of the king's inherent and determinate prerogative in this point, than that *verbal order* of Henry 8. to the lord Grey, governor of Bullen in France, who, upon a dispute about demolishing a fort, the French were then erecting by the name of Chastilon's garden, contrary to the sense of all the lords of his council expressed *in scriptis* on their part, and on the king's part formally confirmed by an order delivered out in his *own letters*, did nevertheless by a verbal commission only, privately whispered to lord Grey, justify that nobleman in flinging down that work, which act was a manifest breach of the peace with the French, and consequently would have been a capital crime in the governor, had not the king had an inherent power in himself at all times and upon all occasions, to break or make leagues or truces, either *per se* or *per deputationem*.

With our law concurs the learned Grotius, *pactione inire* (says he) *quæ bellum finiant, eorum est quorum est bellum; rei enim suæ quisque moderator.* Lib. 3. c. 20. nu. 21.

Livy says, *Fœdera esse, quæ fiunt jussu summæ potestatis.*

Tacitus, of the emperor: *donec referantur literæ, an paci annueret.*

Seneca: *Imperator fœdus percussit, videtur populus Romanus percussisse, & fœdere, continetur.*

*In regnis, regnum est fœdus facere*, says another.

---

## 9 Prerogative.

### *Power of sending and receiving Ambassadors.*

IT is the law of all countries, that messengers of peace, and such as are employed to procure and maintain amity, ought to be defended against all injuries, to be safe and secure in the places where they reside. Now who can be a competent person to receive such negotiators, but he that can afford them safe conduct? and

Jus mittendi legatos, et recipiendi.

and who can perform that, but he that hath authority to inflict penalties on thoſe that dare offer violence unto ſuch ſacred perſonages? and none can inflict puniſhment, but his majeſty, who is the ſovereign, life, and head of the law; and therefore *Jus Legationum* belongs only to the dignity and royal eſtate of the imperial crown of England.

The proofs intended for theſe prerogatives are theſe.

Cam. Eliz anno. f. 41. in Engliſh Co. 4. Inſt. f. 153.

*Nulli niſi Abſoluti Principes & qui majeſtatis Jura habent, legatos conſtituere poſſunt*, (ſays Mr. Cambden) none but abſolute princes, and ſuch as have the prerogative of majeſty can conſtitute ambaſſadors.

Co. 4. Inſt. f. 155.

Of ancient time, and until later days (ſays Coke) no ambaſſador came into this realm, before he had a ſafe conduct from the king: for as no king can come into this realm, without licenſe or ſafe conduct, ſo no Prorex, who repreſenteth the king's perſon, can do it.

1. H. 7. 10. a.

Huſſey ſaid, that in the time of K. Ed. 4. a legate from the pope came to Calais, with an intent to come into England; but the king would not ſuffer him to come into this realm, untill he had taken an oath, that he ſhould attempt nothing againſt the king or his crown. That this was the ancient law of England, appears in our Cambden's Eliz. Anno 1561.

To receive ambaſſadors, Curtius tells us, that it was king-like.

*Et priſtina quidem Regia ſpecies manebat; nam & legati gentium Regem adibant, & copiarum duces aderant, & veſtibulum ſatellites, armatique compleverant.*

10. Pre-

## 10 Prerogative.

### *The power of coyning money.*

THE coining of money is a prerogative of sovereign power, and reckoned amongst the Regalia's of the crown; hence is it, that no money can be currant, but by the king's authority; and in case any subject presume of his own head to coin money, he incurs the heinous crime of high treason: and as it is his majesty's right to make money; so it is his prerogative to make any foreign coin currant within his dominions, by his royal proclamation.

Jus cudendi seu potestas monetandi.

The authorities to be produced for proof of this prerogative are such as these:

It doth appertain to the king only to put a value to the coin, and make the price of the quantity, and to put a print to it, which being done, the coin is currant for so much.

Plow. Com. 316. vide Davy's Reports le case de mizt monies.

The money of England is the treasure of England, and none is said to be treasure-trove, but gold and silver; and this is the reason, the law doth give to the king mines of gold and silver.

Co. 2. Inst. 577.

To counterfeit the king's coin, is declared high treason, by 25 Ed. 3. c. 2. *de proditionibus.*

Also counterfeiting, impairing, &c. of the king's coin, or foreign coin made current, is made high treason, by the 14 Eliz. c. 3, 4. and 18 Eliz. c. 1, 7.

Resolved, that Spanish silver was lawful money of England by proclamation, in the time of Phil. and Mary, and so were French crowns: for the king by his proclamation may make any foreign coin lawful money of England. This prerogative is purely imperial, and so uncontrolled that we find some of our kings have imposed on us copper, others Tinn, and Henry 8. when at Bulloigne in France, issued out leather money, making it as current as silver or gold; nor have any of our kings at any time communicated this privilege to any of their subjects (though some of them have had even the title of KING conferred on them) but have always

Co. Lit. 207. lib. 5. Wade's case.

always kept this power in their own hands, as one of the great *inseparabilia*, not to be parted with.

With our law goes hand in hand the law imperial.

*Jus cudendæ monetæ, nisi cui ab imperatore concessum fuerit, nemo usurpato.*

Budelius de re nummariâ. lib. 1. c. 5. *Monetam seu nummos cudere, non cujusvis est, non privati, non cujusvis civitatis, sed ejus tantum, qui magistratum gerit. Id enim jus inter regalia jura censetur.* Gothofr. *Princeps ad arbitrium suum, irrequisito assensu subditorum valorem monetæ constituere potest, quia populus, quantum ad hoc, omnem potestatem, & jurisdictionem in imperatore transtulisse dicitur.*

---

## 11. Prerogative.

### *The power of Ennobling.*

Jus nobilitandi. AS the beams of the sun spread themselves in giving light, heat, and comfort unto all living creatures without any diminution of the solar virtue, either in substance, course, or brightness, so from the sacred power and royal authority of the kings and queens of England, all dignities do proceed; yet their own princely and sovereign power, *in suâ primâ sublimitate*, doth not suffer or sustain any blemish or detriment.

Co. 4. Inst. 243. The proofs for this prerogative are such as these:

From the royal dignity of the king, all other subordinate dignities, *tanquam lumen de lumine* are derived, without any diminution.

Co. lib. 12. countess of Shrewsbery's case. All honour and nobility is derived from the king, as the true fountain.

Co. Litt. 165 a lib. 12. f. 12. The king is the sovereign of honour and dignity, and therefore if a baron dies having issue divers daughters, the king may confer the dignity on him who marries any of them.

Sir Edw. Terril's case. 14. Caren prized. So in like manner, none may surrender, give up, transfer or part with the honour, degree, title, or dignation majesty hath given or impressed upon him to any person whatsoever; but it must necessarily return to the same royal fountain, from which it first took its it's creation, and that by matter of record; as in the case of a Baronet.

As it appertaineth to the king to confer titles of honour, so at the common law, the king by his prerogative royal, might give such honour, and placing or precedance to his councellors and other his subjects, as should seem good to his royal wisdom. Co.4.Inst. 361. 31. H.8.c.10.

With our common law concurs the civil law: *inter nobiles primus est imperator, cum omnis ordo ab ipso pendeat, ordinis cujusque arbitrium primo est penes imperatorem.* Zoucheus pars 2. sect. 2. de nobilitate

*Princeps ingenuum facere potest, potest & nobilem facere, & ut galli loquuntur,* Il peut faire d'un villein, un chivalier. Gothofredus ad D. 2.4.10.2.

---

## 12. Prerogative.

### *The supreme care and superintendancy in Church-matters, is vested in the King.*

THE highest prerogative (seeing it is purely spiritual) is the *jus rerum sacrarum*, to which no princes in the world have a fairer pretence than ours. For the kings of England are the only kings in all Christendom, that can boast an originally distinct and national church. And though our kings never at any time exercised the sacerdotal function, by performing divine worship in the church, yet they were from time immemorial the rightful *overseers* (Επισκοποι) touching all ecclesiastical supremacy and jurisdiction; and accordingly took upon them to repress the novelties of schisms and corrupt opinions, to reform the indecencies and confusions in sacred administrations, and to DEFEND the church of England against all sacrilegious, invasions upon her rights and revenues. Jus rerum sacrarum penes regem.

It is a gross error to think our kings claim the title of *Defender of the Church or Faith*, from no higher æra than the reign of Henry 8. for we find it in common use with us, three hundred years before that reign, as appears by several writs of king Richard 2. to the sheriffs: the old stile runs thus, "*Fidei cujus nos Defensor sumus, et volumus,*" nor was this a title newly assumed by Richard the 2d. for Constantine the Great, (son of Constantine Chlorus both emperors, both natives of Britain) first took the title of *Defensor Fidei*, (a thousand year before the last mentioned reign) reserving to himself and in himself, all spiritual as well as temporal power.

Matthew, (sirnamed Parker) archbishop of Canterbury, a prelate of great erudition, and deeply skilled in the knowledge of antiquity, published a book in Latin 1573, where he affirms in these express words that "*Rex Angliæ olim erat conciliorum ecclesiasticorum præses vindex temeritatis Romanæ, propugnatur religionis, nec ullam habebant episcopi authoritatem præter eam quam a rege referebant. Jus testamenti probandi non habebant, administrationis potestatem cuiq. delegare non peterant.*"

Now, because the supremacy, *in ecclesiasticis*, is so nice a point as the popish faction render it, many of whom not comprehending the legality, (for who so blind as those who will not see) much less the necessity of its being intrusted with the king only; it may be reasonable to examine the matter of right by the matter of fact, as that by common usage, which our common lawyers date, *du temps d'ont il ny à de memoire au contraire*, from the authority of which age, we may conclude the practice, whatever it has-been, to have gained the form and effect as well as the honour and repute of a law, according to that known maxim, *quod prius est tempore, potius est jure.*

Bracton, fol. 314. Cook sur Lit. l. 2. sect. 170. Cook sur Lit. l. 3. sect. 659.

Pass we then through those four noted periods of Christianity: 1. From the time of Cymbeline anno 156 the first professed believer in the Christian persuasion of any prince in the known world, on which account his countrymen changed his name into that of Levermawer, *i. e.* the *Great Light*; for which reason also, the Romans called him Lucius; a name (as one of our historians figuratively observes) that seems to have been written with the beams of the sun, to the intent it might be legible throughout all ages, to that of Constantine, the first Christian king, or emperor of the Romans, reckoned about a hundred and fifty years. 2. From that time till the conversion of Ethelbert, the first Christian king of the Saxons or English,' supposed to be three hundred and sixty years more.

3. From

3. From that period to the time of the first king of the Norman line here, which was not so little as five hundred years more, at what time the pope first put in his claim. 4. From thence to the time he let go his hold again, which was about the beginning of queen Elizabeth's reign (whose ambassador the Romish pontiff refused to treat with) making up near five hundred years more, and if in all that long series of christianity, it shall appear by consent of all ecclesiastical writers, in all times, that our king has ever been deemed to be *papa patriæ, jure proprietatis*; *& Vicarius Dei in Regno, jure possessionis*; I hope then the imputation of heresy and schism laid upon Henry the eight by Paul the third, for taking upon him to be the supreme head of the church within his own dominions, will vanish as a result of ignorance or prejudice, and our present kings be judged in remitter to their antient right, or (as the law-books express it) *Ensom melior Droit*.

Cymbeline, otherwise Lucius, and those claiming immediately from, by, and after him, I take to be stated in a double right: *rationes fundationis, & ratione donationis*. For (as the lawyers have it) *cujus est dare ejus est disponere*: now that all the bishopricks of this isle were of Cymbeline's foundation and donative, appears by all ecclesiastical historians. And he first reduced the rudiments of the Christian Religion into practice, as divers of our ecclesiastical writers inform us, by establishing with his royal authority, archbishops and bishops in the church; instead of the Roman Flamins and Arch-Flamins, who, before his time, were the chief officers in the Paganish temples, and by this institution, the British church had the start of all other Christian churches in the world, in point of honour, as well as order, seeing it is universally allowed there is no constat of so high a title as that of Archbishop, in any of the Eastern churches at that time. Thus the first Christian canons received their sanction *ex Divinitate Principis* (as the canonists express it) till such time as that foundation laid by him was buried in the rubbish of Dioclesian's persecution. After which we have no proof of any ecclesiastical polity till the time of Constantine, who, having recovered the church out of its ruins, and laid a new superstructure of his own upon the old foundation, is upon that account, both by Eusebius and Socrates

25 Assis. pl. 4. 35 Assis. pl. 11. 23 Edw. 3. 69. 11 Cen. 4. 50. Tit. Remit. 11.

Euseb. vit. Constant. cap. 24. l. 4. Socrat. hist. Eccles.

ſtiled the Great (and it is well they called him not the Univerſal) Biſhop: his power being no leſs extenſive than his dominions; the firſt of them pointing at his power in general, calls him τὸν ὑπὸ Θεȣ̃ Καθιςάμενον Ἐπίσκοπον; the laſt referring to his more immediate power over the clergy (for to ſay truth, he precided even in Rome itſelf) ſtiles him Ἐπίσκοπον τῶν Ἐπισκόπων, *i. e. Epiſcopus Epiſcoporum*, or, in other words, *Pontifex Maximus.*

Sygenius lib. 9. de Reg. Italiæ dicit, non debere Ambroſianum Rom. legibus ſubjicere.

From the time of this Conſtantine the Great, till that of pope Gregory the Great, neither heard the natives or churchmen of Britain, any thing of the church of Rome, nor they of Rome any thing of the church of Britain; nor will this aſſertion ſeem ſtrange, when we reflect, that Rome was at that time but a private dioceſs, not having credit enough to give laws even to all the churches of Italy, much leſs to impoſe any upon thoſe further off; for every perſon of literature knows that Millanees (not to mention any other) conteſted with the Romans for the precedence many years after: and as a farther and inconteſtible proof it is indiſputably known, that as ſoon as Auſtin came hither, he found part of this iſle Pagans and part Chriſtians; but the latter ſeemed to him to be more inhoſpitable than the other; at leaſt, they were ſo far from ſubmitting to his legatine authority after the ignorant Pagans had owned it, that they fell from arguments to arms, and the miſſionary having no probability of ſubjugating

He cauſed 1200 Monks of the Britains to be murthered at one time.

them under his juriſdiction, baptized almoſt as many of them in blood as he did in water; but as it appeared that he brought them no new faith, ſo neither would they ſuffer him to bring in any new laws amongſt them, defending their own church ſo well with their own cannons, that neither he, nor any of the Roman community could break in upon them, or infringe their liberty in the leaſt for the ſpace of near five hundred years, when Henry the ſecond, reducing both ſtate and church under like paction of ſervitude, forced them by the laws of conqueſt to part as well from their eccleſiaſtical as civil rights; and at the ſame time they became no church, to become no people, being ſo cantonized with England, that they were no longer conſiderable; which had yet been impoſſible for him

to

to have effected, had he not at the same time he set up his own, declared against the pope's supremacy.

But to proceed to that of the Britains, to consider the primitive state of the English church, it may yet be allowed for good prescription (and that we know is a title implies a long continued and peaceable possession derived *ab authoritate legis)* if it can be made out that any of the Saxon kings, converted by the aforesaid Austin from the time of the proto-christian king Ethelbert himself, until the Norman conquest, did at any time so far agnize the pope's authority, as to forbear the exercise of any part of that spiritual dominion which they challenged *proprio jure*. For as it is evident that they did constrain as well ecclesiasticks as laicks to submit to the final determination, as well of spiritual as civil pleas in their temporal courts, so they not seldom made the ecclesiastical censures without, and sometimes against the consent of the bishop, if it displeased them, even after excommunication pronounced: nor did they dispense even with the offences themselves, if they were only *mala per accidens*, and not *mala in se* (as the casnists distinguish.) Nay, they did not permit even nuns to marry against the usual practice of those times, and the judgment of the church, doing many other things of the like nature, which whoso reads *M. Paris*, *Florentius Eadmerus*, &c. will find more at large than becomes the brevity I design; and all this they did without any exception or scandal, or, (to use Baronius his own phrase) *sine ulla Ecclesiarum Labe*.

Lit. sect. 170.

Leg. Alfred cap. 8 p. 25.

As were priest marriage, basturdy, non residency, pluralities &c.

Baronius tome 3. anno 312. N. 100.

Indeed such was the plentitude of their ecclesiastical power, that each king of them was (as the priest prayed at their coronation they might be) *sicut Aaron in tabernaculo, Zacharias in templo, Petrus in Clave*; as appears by their several edicts yet extant; some for the better observation of the lord's day, some for the due keeping of Lent, others for the right administration of the Sacraments, the regulation of matrimony, and ascertaining the degrees of consanguinity, some for permitting divorces, others for perfecting contracts; in fine, they did whatever might become the wisdom and honour of such as had the sole care of the church, all christian obedience being enforced *providentiâ & potentiâ regis* (as Hoveden expresses it) or as we find it

See the old formular continued till H. 6. time.

Leg. alured. c. 39. p. 33.

Bede lib. 3 cap. 8.

Jornal, 1. 761. c. 2.

Leg. Canut, c. 7. p. 101. Leg. alured, ut supra. Hoveden fol. 410. 2 H. 4. N. 44. Bellarm. Pontif. lib. 4. Twisden eccles. jurisd. Regis. Jan. Anglor. lib. 1. pag. 85.

it in some records, *justitiâ & fortitudine regis*; for however the bishop was always joined in commission with the lay magistrate, as having in him *jus ordinis* (as some divines call it) yet this was not so much in affirmation of his ecclesiastical as for prevention of his disputing the regal authority, and to take off all clashing, *inter placita regis & christianitatis jura*, that is to say, in M. Paris's own words, *ne contra regiam coronam, & dignitatem aliquid statuere tentaret Episcoput*, who was to the king as the arch-deacon to him *tanquam oculus regis*, as the other was *tanquam oculus episcopi*.

But the greatest instance of all was, that of the investiture of the bishops by the king; who gave them the ring and the pastoral staffe, the antient emblems of supream dignity and authority, which he himself had accepted at his coronation: the first signifying the power of joining such an one to the church; the last denoting the jurisdiction ecclesiastical, in *foro interiori*, or as some term it, *in foro animæ*; but he kept the scepter in his own hand as the proper ensign of that *jus potentiæ*, or sovereign power, by which he stood particularly obliged to *defend* the church; to which king Edgar doubtless referred when he told his bishops at a genaral convocation, *ego Constantini, vos Petri gladium habetis in manibus*; and as Christ commanded Peter, as soon as he had drawn his sword to put it up again; so did he (as Christ's representative) forbid St. Dunstan (who would be thought St. Peter's) to sheath his weapon when he began to draw upon the lay magistrate, and would have been medling with those things that were Τὰ Ἐκτὸς τῆς Ἐκκλησίας, forbidding any inquiry to be made, *de peccatis subditoram*: add to this that in all general councils the king himself presided *tanquam papa patriæ*; thus Ina (for I chuse to begin with him, because Baronius stiles him *Rex maximæ pius*) presided in the great synod at Winchester, *anno* 733, by the title of *Vicarius Dei*. Edgar, at another meeting gave the law to all the clergy, *tanquam pastor pastorum*; the like did Ethelred under the stile of *Vicarius Christi*; after him again Canute presided in another council at Winchester by the title of *Dei Præco* once, and another time at Southampton, under the stile of *Divini Juris Interpres*; neither was Edward the confessor behind any of them, when he made his ecclesiastical

As Socrates expresses it.

Tom. 9. anno 740. N. 14. Jornal, lib. 761. Vide Tit. Gar. Edgar Eadmer, 246, 10.

cleſiaſtical laws by the title of *Vicarius Summi Regis*. Theſe titles I have the rather mentioned to ſhew what divine office was eſteemed to be in the king properly, who having a mixture of the prieſt and prophet with that of his kingſhip, was obliged to be ſolicitous, *tam de ſalute animarum, quam de ſtatu regni*, as Jarvalenſis expreſſes it; and thus our wiſe law-makers heretofore (not to ſay law-maſters) who were very nice in wording all the antient ſtatutes relating to the ſupremacy, have not ſtiled the king a ſpiritual perſon (although they knew him to be 'Επιστημονάρχης) but *perſona mixta cum Sacerdote*.

Eadmer, 155, 6. Leg. Canut, l. 26. p. 106. Leg. Ed. confeſ. c. 17. p. 142. Leg. Inæ. in prefat. p. 1. apud Jorvalenſ. col. 761. 41.

And accordingly it is well argued by Dr. South, a writer of no mean note, that his authority muſt be equivalent with any of thoſe popes, at leaſt, who were laicks at the time they were choſen to that supream dignity. For, whilſt there is no qualification in their office of papacy to render them ſo far eccleſiaſtical as to conſecrate any biſhop perſonally, but that of neceſſity they muſt do it (as he notes) by their bull; it muſt neceſſarily follow, that that bull (being a deputation granted to ſome biſhop to do the office for him) differs very little, if any thing from that of the king's commiſſion in the like caſe. And if it had been otherwiſe underſtood in former times, it had been in the power of his Unholineſs to have extinguiſhed the function of biſhops in any princes dominions whatever.

Vid. lib. intit. animadvert upon the book intit. Fanaticiſm Fanatically imputed to the catholic church by Dr. S.

The firſt pope who found out a way to ſupplant the king's authority *in eccleſiaſticis*, by ſeeming to ſupport it, was Nicholas the ſecond, one of the moſt ſubtil of all the Roman prelates, contemporary with Edward the confeſſor, one of the weakeſt of our kings; who created a title to himſelf by implication, whilſt he perſuaded the king to accept of a bull of confirmation ſtom him, by which granting him, *Plenam advocationem regni & omnium totius Angliæ Eccleſiarum*; he made that ſeem to be of grace only from him, which before was of right in the king: of which artifice his ſucceſſor Gregory the ſeventh, took no ſmall advantage, when he put in for a ſhare of the ſupremacy with William the *Baſtard*, making that *ſingle* preſident the foundation of his claim. 1. *The inveſtiture of biſhops*, which I take to be that *directum dominium* held by the king, *jure patronatus*; in acknowledgement of which right, the clergy

Vid Twiſden ut ſupra.

clergy pay him their * first fruits. 2. The benefit of *Annates*, which was a chief rent out of all the spiritualities. 3. The power of *Calling Synods*, by which he might impose upon the government. 4. The right of † *Receiving Appeals* to *Rome*; which overthrew all the king's courts. 5. The sole power of ‡ disposing and translating bishops, which made them his homagers and feifes. 6. The power of *altering* and *dispensing with Canons*. 7. The privilege of *sending a legate* to reside here; as a spiritual spy to detect all the secrets of state, and be a kind of check-mate to the king himself.

But William the *Bastard*, as he was a prince that was apter to invade other men's rights, than to part with any of his own: so finding his prerogative sufficiently guarded by the antient laws of the land, then called The laws of king Edward, (which was not the least reason he continued so many of them as he did) would by no means yield to him so long as he lived: his son William Rufus continuing yet more obstinate, who, after the death of the aforesaid Gregory, surnamed Hildebrand, would admit of no pope, but what himself approved of: so that for eleven years together there was no pope acknowledged here in England; which may be a good president for any churchman that shall hereafter hold (as some of their catholick doctors have as far as they durst affirm) that there may be *Auferibilitas Papæ*; neither would he permit appeals or any intercourse to Rome; which when Anselme archbishop of Canterbury (who was a natural Italian) attempted to bring about, he first rifled him and then banished him: neither was his brother Henry the first less tenacious of his right, as appears by those instructions given to his bishops when they went to meet Calixt the second at the council of Reimes; whom he forbad in the first place to appeal to the pope upon any grievance whatever, for that himself (he said) would be sole judge betwixt them. 2. He commanded them to tell the pope plainly, if he expected his antient

See Dr. Dun 43 Sermon preached on the 5th Nov. at Pauls cross

* First fruits and annates, an. 1534, 26. H. 8. c. 3. were granted to the king. † Suing an appeal to Rome is made treason, 13 El. c. 8. ‡ No man to be presented to the see of Rome, for the dignity of bishop, &c. 25 H. 8. c. 10.

rent

rent here, he would expect a confirmation of his antient priviledges. 3. He directed them to salute the pope and receive his apostolick precepts, *sed superfluas inventiones regno meo inferre nolite.* The contest between the arch bishop Becket, and Henry the second, shews what temper he was of: for he opposed both the pope and the bishop so long, that they had undoubtedly cast him out of the church, but that they feared he would not come in again: only king John, in a kind of distraction that was upon him, when wrackt betwixt two extreams of hate and fear, (his enemies pressing hard upon him, whilst his friends forsook him) to avoid being split upon either rock, cast himself upon the quick sand of the pope *Innocent* the third's protection, submitting to an act of pennance that shewed the weakness of his faith more than of his right, his renouncing the supremacy at that time, being no more to be wondered at than his renouncing christianity itself at another time; but his son recover'd the ground his father lost, when he brought the whole kingdom to resent the indignity so far, as to join with him in demanding satisfaction of the same pope, and not content with a bare disclaimer, forced the insolent legate to fly the kingdom, *timens pelli sui* (as the record hath it) neither stopt the parliament there, but voting that submission of his father a breach of his coronation oath, entered so far into the consideration of the whole matter of the pope's usurpation, as to make that statute of proviso's, which after brought in those other 27 and 38 Edw. 3. and that brought on the treaty betwixt that king and Gregory the Eleventh, which after two years debate ended with this express agreement, *Quod papa de caetero reservationibus beneficiorum minime uteretur*, which dignities Henry the fourth, made no scruple to collate to his own use, notwithstanding his being anointed with that oil which came from heaven, whose virtue was to incline all the princes that were inaugurated with it to be favourable to the church: his son Henry the Fifth (for his exemplary piety stiled the Prince of Priests) thought fit to demand of Martin the Fifth several ecclesiastical priviledges, which his predecessors had got from the kings of England at several times, and his ambassadors finding the pope to stick at it, and give them no ready answer, told him plainly, that the king their master intended to use his own

Walsingham hist. 1374. p. 184.

mind in the matter, whether he consented or no, *Ut pete quæ non à necessitatis sed honoris causa petat.*

In vit. II. Chichley. p. 56, 57. Edito. an. 1617.

Thus the papal power as it was interrupted in all times, so from this time it sensibly languished, till it received its fatal blow from Henry the Eighth, who (if I may so say) did, as it were beat out the pope's brains with his own keys; and had he not afterward used violence to himself, by referring the point of his supremacy to the parliament, to be confirmed by statute law, that was sufficiently firmed before by the common law, that cannot change, he had undoubtedly been more absolute lord of himself than any christian prince whatever, and acknowledged head of the church, *nullis exceptionibus* (as Tacitus expresses it in another case:) but laying the burthen of that weighty question of the supremacy upon the shoulders of divines, which had been better supported by those of the great lawyers, he was perplext with many scruples, and in the end forced to enter the list in person, and fight the pope at his own weapon, the pen; in which combat, (by great good fortune, being a great master of defence that way) he had the better of it, and by the authority of his example drew many to second him; so that his supremacy was afterwards justified by the whole convocation of divines in both the universities, and most of the monastics and collegiate theologists of the whole kingdom, four only excepted, who adventured to assent the pope's right.

Antiqu. Brit. Ecclef p.384 37.

I shall now observe by way of recapitulation and further explanation, that all the ecclesiastical laws of England, were not derived, nor brought from the court of Rome: for, a long time before the canon law was authorized and published (which was since the Norman line) the ancient kings of this realm, Ina, Alfred, Edward, Athelstan, Edmund, Edgar, Canutus, and Edward the confessor, have by the advice of their own clergy, within the realm, made divers ordinances for the government, of the church of England. *Vide* our Saxon laws, by Mr. Lambard.

Vid. Davy's Rep. Le case de commen. la.

And since the coming of William the Norman, provincial synods have been held, and many constitutions have been made by William the first. H. 1. Ed. 1. *&c.* all which are part of our ecclesiastical laws to this day, unless

unless altered or repealed by statute law. And therefore the kings of England from time to time in every age, have granted dispensations in ecclesiastical affairs, as we find them amply testified by the charters of Kenulphus, and William the Norman, sirnamed the *Bastard*. Co. lib. 5. Cawdry's case.

Besides, many of those ecclesiastical laws now here in force, are not laws derived from the pope, but were extracted out of the ancient canons, as well general as national. *Vide* Davy's Reports, 72. b. 73. a Le case de Commenda. Anderson's Reports, Evans and Ascough's case. Co. lib. 4. Holland's case.

And farther; although some of the pope's canons, are here received (I deny they were imposed,) and used in this realm, yet by such an allowance, reception and usage, they became part of the ecclesiastical laws of this nation: and for this cause the interpretation, dispensation and execution of those canons, belong only to the kings of England and their ministerial and judicial officers within their own dominions; and the king of England and his judges have the sole jurisdiction in such cases, and the bishop of Rome has nothing to do in the interpretation, or execution of those laws within the king's dominions, although they were first devised at Rome, no more than the chief magistrates of Athens or Lacedæmon could claim jurisdiction in the ancient city of Rome, because the laws of the twelve tables were brought from those cities of Greece: no more say I, than the master of New Colledge in Oxford, shall have command and jurisdiction over King's Colledge in Cambridge, because, the private statutes by which King's Colledge is governed, were for the most part taken out of the foundation-book of New Colledge in Oxford: and certainly by the same reason the emperor may claim jurisdiction in maritime causes within the dominions of the king of England, because we have received and admitted the use of the imperial laws, for a long time, for the determination of naval causes.

I say further, seeing several of the pope's canons were rejected by temporal princes. As for example:

1. The canon that prohibited the donation of benefices *per manum Laicum*, was always disobeyed in England, France, Naples, and divers other countries.

2. The canon to make infants legitimate, which were born before espousals, was particularly rejected in this realm; when in a parliament held at *Merton omnes comites, & barones una voce responderunt; nolumus leges Angliæ mutari, quæ huc usque usitatæ sunt.* 20 H. 3. c. 9. Co. 2. Inst. f. 98. Co. Lit. 245. a.

3. The canon that exempted clerks from secular power, was never fully observed in any kingdom of Christendom.

4. The canon that ousteth battle in a writ of right, was not here received.

5. The king of England and his council, did not receive the constitution of the bishop of Rome, at Lyons, which excluded men twice married, or Bigamy, from all privilege of clergy.

Seeing, I say, such canons as these were rejected; it is an argument undeniable, that those canons or constitutions, had not their force from any authority which the court of Rome had to impose laws on the English kings; for, by the very same reason they rejected the canons above mentioned, they might have rejected all others that were received.

---

## 13. Prerogative.

### *The highest and last Appeal appertaineth to his Majesty.*

Extremæ provocationis jus. THE dignity royal of England being not feudatory to the majesty of any other prince, as to a superior lord, but imperial, and independant; our king hath plenary power and jurisdiction, to put a final determination to all causes whatsoever, without provocation to any foreign potentate; and therefore from his majesty's sentence lieth no manner of appeal.

The proofs for this prerogative are these:

Doctor & Stu. lib. 2. c. 36 The king and his progenitors, kings of England, without time of mind have had authority to determine the right of patronages in this realm in their own courts, and are bound to see, that their subjects have right in that

that behalf within the realm; and in that case from him lieth no appeal.

At the parliament holden at Clarendon, it was enacted and declared, *that no appeals should be made to the court of Rome*. 10 H. 2. c. 8.

It is declared in 24 H. 8. That the king is instituted by the goodness of God, with entire power, to yield justice, and *final* determination of all subjects within this realm in all causes without restraint or provocation to any foreign potentate of the world. 24 H. 8. c. 12.

A general prohibition in 25 H. 8. that no one shall be pursued out of the realm to Rome, or elsewhere. 25 H. 8. c. 19.

Our law, (says Sir Jo. Davis) in his preface dedicatory, doth demonstrate the strength of wit and reason, and self sufficiency, which hath been always in the people of the land, which have made their own laws out of their wisdom and experience, not begging or borrowing a common-wealth from Rome, or from Greece, as all other nations of Europe, but having sufficient provision of law and justice within the land, and have need *justitiam & judicium ab alienigenis emendicare*.

Note, my lord Coke says, that though the statutes of 24 and 25 H. 8. do upon certain appeals make the sentence definitive, as to any appeal; yet the king after such definitive sentence, as supreme head, may grant a commission *ad revidendum*, because that after a sentence definitive, the pope, as pretended supreme head, by the canon law used to grant a commission to review, and such authority as the pope had *de facto*, doth of right belong to the crown, and is annexed unto it by the statutes of 26 H. 8. c. 1. and 1 Eliz. c. 1. Co 4. Inst. fo. 341.

That the last appeal belongs to the sovereign power, Tacitus can tell us in the fourth book of his Annals; *Iisque instantibus ad principem provocant*; and Agrippa, who said unto Festus, *This man might have been set at liberty, if he had not appealed unto Cæsar.*

## 14. Prerogative.

### *The power of Founding Colledges, Guildes, and Fraternities.*

Poteſtas collegia & univerſitates inſtituendi. King is ſaid in our law never to die.

AS it is the ſole power of almighty god to create natural perſons, ſo 'tis a privilege royal in his majeſty, to found bodies politick, to give them life and being, to make them (like himſelf) immortal. Hence no corporation (be it temporal or eccleſiaſtical) can be erected within this realm to continue in ſucceſſion, and to be capable of endowments without the authority and licenſe of his moſt excellent majeſty.

The authorities to back this prerogative are theſe:

9 H. 6. 16 b.

The king only may grant a licenſe to found a ſpiritual corporation.

Co. lib. 4. adam's and lamberts caſe. 107. b. Co. 3. Inſt 202.

The pope cannot found or incorporate a colledge within this realm, neither can he aſſign or licenſe others to give temporal livings to it; but it ought to be done by the king himſelf, and no other.

Altho the baronage of England might build churches without the kings licenſe; yet could they not erect a ſpiritual politick body to continue in ſucceſſion, without the king's licenſe.

Any man may erect, and build an houſe for an hoſpital, ſchool, working-houſe, or houſe of correction, or the like, without any licenſe: for that it is but a preparation, and may be done as owner of the ſoil, but by the common-law, could not incorporate any of them without the royal licenſe.

Co. 3. Inſt 202.

49 Aſſpel. 8. le caſe de Whit tawers.

The cuſtom of London to make corporations, was held void: for the king only can do it by his prerogative.

Coke lib. 8. f. 125. The caſe of don.

In favour of trade, the law giveth the king power to erect Guildam Mercatoriam, a fraternity, ſociety, and incorporation of merchants.

Every body politick or corporate, be it eccleſiaſtical or lay, may commence and be eſtabliſhed three manner of ways, viz. by preſcription, by letters patents, or by act of parliament; and to any of theſe ways is the

the royal assent, allowance, and approbation necessary.

The civil law runs thus: *Neque Societates, neque Collegium, neque hujusmodi Corpus passim omnibus habere conceditur. Collegia autem certa sunt, quorum corpus constitutionibus principalibus conservatum est.* D. 3. 4. 1. *Collegium, si nullo speciali privilegio subnixum sit, hæreditatem capere non posse, dubium non est. Cod.* 6. 24. 8.

---

## 15. Prerogative.

### *Power of dispensing with Politick Laws.*

NO act of parliament can bind the king from any prerogative, that is solely and inseparably annext to his sacred person, and royal power; but that he may dispense with it, by a *non obstante*. Jus dispensandi.

As for example; it is provided by the statute of 23 H. 6. c. 8. That all patents made of any office of a sheriff for term of years, or for life, in fee simple, or in taile, are void and of none effect, any clause or word of *Non obstante*, in any wise put in such patents to be made, notwithstanding; yet the king by his royal sovereign power of commanding, may command any person by his patent to serve him and the weal publick, as sheriff of such a county, for years, or for life, &c. with a special *non obstante*, contrary to the statute, which pretendeth to exclude *non obstantes*. 2. H. 7. 6. 6. 13 H. 7. 8. b. Plowd. Com. Grendon. v. bishop of Lincoln. 205. 6.

So none shall be a justice of assize as appears by the statute of 8. R. 2. c. 2. in the county where he was born, or did inhabit, and yet the king, with a special *non obstante* may dispense with this law; for this dispensation belongs to the inseparable prerogative of the king, viz. his power of commandment to serve. 8. R. 2. c. 2.

To what I have said, relating to this prerogative, I will subjoin certain rules, by which the reader may the better discern for the future, the true extent and latitude of the king's dispensative power; that is to say, with what he can, and with what he may not dispense. And my rules are such as these:

1. When

1. When an act of parliament is made that disableth any person, or maketh any thing void or tortious for the good of the church or commonwealth, in this law all the subjects have an interest, and the king himself may not dispense with it (no more than with the common law. As for instance.

It was resolved by sir Thomas Egerton lord chancellor of England, and Coke upon conference with other judges, upon a question referred unto them by king James: That one sir Robert Vernon cofferer to the king, having contracted with sir Arthur Jugram for money to assign his office; and sir Arthur having obtained a grant of it from the king; It was, I say, resolved that the bargain by the statute of 5 Ed. 6.c.1.6. was void, and that the person (sir Arthur,) was disabled to take that office, as at no time during his life, he can have it, although it become void, by the death of any other officer, and a new grant be made unto him, with a *non obstante* of the statute aforesaid. Co. 1. Inst. 234. a. Co. 3. Inst. 154. Cro. 2. part 386. The king v. bishop of Norwich. Hobarts reports Roy v. bishop of Norwich f. 75.

As the king may not dispense with the statute of 5. E. 6. nor with the statutes, viz. of 3. E. 4. c. 4. of manufactures, Co. lib. 11. Monopolies f. 8. 15. R. 2. c. 3. of the admiral jurisdiction Hill. 7. Jac. Hiemaus case. 31. Eliz. c. 6. of simony Co. 3. Inst. 154. Co. Litt. 120. a. Hobart f. 75. 5. Eliz. c. 1. of knights for taking the oath of supremacy. Co. 3. Inst. 154.

2. When a statute prohibiteth any thing upon a corporal pain, there the king may dispense with the penalty. As for example, if any man transports wool beyond sea, to any other place, besides the staple, it shall be felony; in this case the king may license a man to do it, and he shall not be impeached of it, and so 'tis of all other like forfeitures given to the king, 13. H. 7. 8. b. 11. H. 7. 12. a. Vide. Co. 3. Inst. f. 74. on the statute of 5. H. 4. c. 4. touching multiplication.

3. Where a statute prohibiteth any thing upon a penalty, and giveth the penalty to the king, or to the king and informer, there the king may dispense with the

the penalty, Co. 1. Inſt. 122. a. Co. lib. 11. the caſe of Monopolies 88. Co. lib. 7. penal laws.

4. No act of parliament can ſo bind the king from any prerogative that is ſolely and inſeparably annexed to his royal perſon and power, but that he may diſpenſe with it by a *non obſtante*, vid. 2. H. 7. 6 b. 13. H. 7. 8. b. *Plowden's Com. Grendon v. L'eveſque de Lincolne* 502. b. Co. lib. 7. Calvin's caſe. Co. lib. 12. fol. 18.

5. And laſt rule is this, when ſtatutes are enacted to put things in ordinary form, and to eaſe our ſovereign of labour, thoſe laws do not ſo deprive him of power, but that he may diſpenſe with them: as for inſtance, the commiſſion of tryal of pyracy upon the ſtatute of 28 H. 8. c. 13. is good, though the chancellor do not nominate the commiſſioners, as that ſtatute appoints, 4 Eliz. Dyer f. 211.

The queen made ſheriffs without the judges, notwithſtanding the ſtatute of 9. E. 2. Mich. 5. &. 6. Eliz. Dyer 225. b.

The office of alnage granted by the queen without the bill of the treaſurer it is good with a *non obſtante* againſt the ſtatute of 31 H. 6. c. 5. for theſe ſtatutes, Mich. 13.
and the like were made to put things in ordinary form, & 14.
and to eaſe the ſovereign of labour, but not to deprive Eliz. Dyer
him of power; and therefore the king is not reſtrained f. 303. b.
by ſuch laws, but his regal authority remains full and perfect as before, and he can diſpenſe with them as king; for all acts of juſtice and grace flow from him.

---

## 16. Prerogative.

### *General Laws bind not the King.*

THE king in reſpect of the dignity and ſuperexcellency of his perſon, is not included within general words, and therefore being not particularized in an act of parliament, is exempted out of it, be the ſtatute in the affirmative, or negative. As for example:

Plow. Com. Berkley's case. The statute of Westm. 2. c. 5. which gives the plea of Plenarty by six months, doth not bind the king, because the act is general, and the king is not named.

So by the statute of *Magna Charta*. c. 11. its provided in the negative, that *Communia placita non sequantur Curiam nostram, sed teneantur in certo aliquo loco*; but this doth not bind the king: for he may have a *Quare impedit*, in the kings-bench; because a general act doth not extend to the king.

part Armiger v. Holland. So the king by his prerogative, may license a new bishop to retain his parsonage in Commendam, notwithstanding negative words in the statute of 25 H. 8. because not expresly named in it.

Vide more of this kind of learning, Plowden's Com. 240. Berkley's Case. 4 & 5 Phil. & Mar. Dyer 155. a. Cro. 3. part. Alcough's Case in the court of wards.

---

## 17. Prerogative.

### *Judges are bound to take notice of all statutes that concern the King, though they be not pleaded.*

IT is due by oath, and office to watch for him, who wakes for us, *nequid detrimenti capiat Respublica*; and if charity begins at it self, so ought justice to do, that his majesty who granteth justice to all, should not be wanting to himself, and therefore 'tis great reason, that the judges, who are conduit pipes and conveyances of the king's justice, should always take cognizance of those laws which advance our sovereigns interest, though they be not pleaded.

In proof of this prerogative, this one authority is offered.

Co.lib. 4. Holland's case. In all acts of parliament, though the matter of them contains individual or particular things; yet if they touch the king, the judges *ex officio*, ought to take cognizance: for every subject has an interest in the king, as the head of the commonwealth; and if the inferiour members cannot estrange themselves of the actions

actions or passions of the head, no less may any subject estrange himself of any thing that concerns the king, their supreme head; and therefore it is, that the law accounts all statutes that concern the king, general laws; and takes notice of them, though they be not pleaded.

Vide more of this learning. Co. lib. 4. Lord Cromwell's Case Co lib. 8. Casus principis 28. a. Plowden's Com. Willion v. Berkley 231.

---

## 18. Prerogative.

*No length of time can weaken, alter, or defeat the Kings interest.*

NEITHER custom nor prescription ought to exalt its self against the kings prerogative, neither can any laws be imputed to him, because it is presumed, that his majesty is always imployed, about the affairs of the kingdom, and has not leisure (as subjects have) to look after his own particular rights and interests, and therefore *vigilantibus & non dormientibus Jura subveniunt* is a rule for the subject; but no prescription or length of time, runneth against the king, nor can bring any prejudice to his royal rights, as for instance.

Custom of London to retain goods pledged, till satisfaction be made, doth not extend to the jewels of the crown; so if a man hath toll or wreck, or stray by prescription, this extends not to the goods of the king.

So if lands (in which the king hath a right to enter) be aliened before the king enter, yet the king may enter into whose hands soever the lands shall come, because *nullum tempus occurrit Regi.*

The reader may meet with more of this kind of learning in Mirror cap. 3. Plowden's Com. f. 243. Co. lib. 6. Boswell's case Co. Litt. 294. b.

35. H. 6. 26. a. Davy's Rep. 33. b. case de Tanistry. Co Litt. Sect. 178. 13. H. 7. 6. 9. H. 6. 21. a.

## 19. Prerogative.

### *The King is Lord Paramount.*

Dominus super omnes.

THE Feudists divide lands, in which a person hath a perpetual estate, into *Feudum & Allodium*; the first is that which a man holds by acknowledgement of superiority and attendance; the latter, defined to be land, that one possesseth in his own right, without any service or duty; this last is a property in the superlative degree, which in this kingdom solely belongeth to his majesty, the lord Paramount; the fountain from which all lands were first derived, and to which they revert upon breach of allegiance, as commitment of treason, &c.

The authorities to be produced in proof of this prerogative, are these:

Bracton, Co. Lit. f. 1. b.

*Prædium domini regis est directum dominium, cujus nullus author est nisi Deus*; and therefore the possessions of the king, are called, *Sacra Patrimonia*, because the king hath no superior, but God Almighty.

Terms of law f. 246. b.

Property is the highest right that a man hath, or can have to any thing, which no way dependeth upon another man's curtesy; and this none in this kingdom can have in any lands or tenements, but only the king in the right of his crown, because that all the lands thro' the realm, are in nature of fee, and are held immediately or mediately of the crown.

Co. Litt. 65. a. 98 a. Co. 4. Inst. 355. Co. 4. inst. 301, 363.

All lands within this realm, (says Sir Edward Coke) were originally derived from the crown; and therefore the king is sovereign lord, or lord Paramount either mediate or immediate of all, and every parcel of land within the realm.

The sovereign lordship of the emperors, was thus described by Seneca, *lib. 7. de beneficiis cap.* 3 & 4. *Omnia rex* (says he) *imperio possidet singuli dominio; ad imperatores potestas omnium pertinet, ad singulos proprietas: in iis est suprema potestas & gubernatio, non proprietas rerum singularum. Vide* Doctor Duck, *lib. 2. c. 1. un. 6. de authoritate juris civilis*, Earl of Clarendon in his survey of chap. 24, of the Leviathan.

20. Pre-

## 20. Prerogative.

*The king for the public good, can deprive a subject of his right.*

THOUGH, since the law of property hath been introduced, every man may challenge this or that to be his own, yet in case of public necessity, for the safety of the kingdom, his majesty may revive that pristine right of using things, as if they still remained in common. This doctrine is founded upon the old rule, *Salus populi, suprema lex est*; wherefore the property of the subject shall not so exclude the royal dominion of our sovereign; but that he lawfully may (in cases of necessity, for the good of the commonweal) use his sovereignty, and supereminent dominion.

As for example; when the enemy comes against the realm, to the sea-coast, it is lawful to come upon any land adjoining to the same coast, to make trenches or bulwarks for the defence of the realm; for every subject hath benefit by it; and in such cases of extremity, they may dig for gravel, for the making of bulwarks; and for the common-wealth a man shall suffer damage, as for saving a city, or town, a house shall be plucked down, if the next be on fire: and the suburbs of a city in the time of war, for the common safety, shall be plucked down. And a thing for the common-wealth every man may do, without being liable to an action; and in this case the rule holds true, *Princeps & respublica ex justa causa possunt rem meam auferre.*

Co. lib. 12. f. 12, & 13. 8 E. 4. 23. 3 H. 8. 15. 21 H. 7. 27. b.

What the supreme power may do in cases of necessity, and public danger, *vide* Mr. Roger Coke's observations on Hugo Grotius, page 48. And in his fourth book of Justice, c. 1. num. 5. Doctor Sanderson in his Prelection the tenth *de obligatione conscientiæ*. How the maxim, *Salus populi, suprema lex*, is to be understood, see Doctor Sanderson's Prelection the tenth, throughout, and the author of that most learned and profound tract, intitled, *Sacro-sancta Regum Majestas*, c. 16.

## 21. Prerogative.

*Goods, in which no man can claim property, belong to the king.*

THOSE things in which no man can claim property do appertain (according to nature) to the firſt occupant. Thus here in England of ancient time, wrecks and other caſualties, as treaſure-trove, waifes, ſtrays, and ſuch like, did belong to the firſt finder; but afterwards the law appointed them to the king, as ſovereign and ſupreme head of the commonwealth.

The authorities for proof of this prerogative, are ſuch as theſe:

Lib. 2. c. 24. nu. 1. *Habet rex* (ſays Bracton) *præ cæteris omnibus in regno ſuo, de jure gentium privilegia propria, quæ de jure naturali eſſe deberent inventoris, ſicut Theſaurus, Wreccum maris, Balæna, ſturgio, waivium, quæ in nullius bonis eſſe dicuntur; ac etiam aliæ res, quæ dominum non habent, ſicut animalia vagantia quæ nullus ſequitur petit vel advocat.*

Lib. 1. c. 43. Fleta thus: *Theſaurus licet inventoris erat, jam de jure gentium, regis efficitur, & alia quædam, quæ in nullius bonis eſſe dicuntur ſicut Wreccum Maris, Balæna, Sturgio, & Waivium.*

8 H.4.2.b All goods in England in which no body has property, are adjudged the king's by his prerogative.

*Vide* more of theſe matters in Bracton, *lib.* 3. *Tract.* 2. *c.* 3. *nu.* 4. *Fleta, lib.* 1. *c.* 45.

22. Prero-

## 22. Prerogative.

*The king is the ſovereign lord, and proprietor of the narrow ſeas.*

THE king of Great-Britain, is the lord and proprietor of the circumfluent, and ſurrounding ſea, as an inſeparable and perpetual appendix of the Britiſh empire; he hath time out of mind enjoyed ſupreme government and juriſdiction, in preſcribing laws for the preſervation of peace and juſtice, in giving rules of navigation to ſuch as paſs through it, in exerciſing all manner of authority in matters of judicature, and in receiving all ſuch profits and commodities as are peculiar to every kind of ſea-dominion whatſoever.

That the king has enjoyed ſeveral ſuper-eminent rights in the Britiſh ſeas, as ſpecial ſigns or pledges of ſovereignty and dominion, ſhall be evidenced by records, and the marks or ſigns are ſuch as theſe.

1. *Making laws and exerciſing ſupreme naval juriſdiction over all perſons, and in all caſes*

Very many foreign nations, as well as the eſtates of England, did in a libel or bill of complaint, publicly exhibit in the time of king Edward the firſt, and king Philip the Fair, before a court of Delegates, eſpecially in that behalf by them appointed, in expreſs terms acknowledge, that the king of England hath ever been lord not only of this ſea, but alſo of the iſlands placed in it *par raiſon du Roialme d' Angleterre*, upon the account of the realm of England, or as they were kings of England, which truly (ſays our Mr. Selden) is all one, as in moſt expreſs terms, to aſcribe this whole ſea unto them, as far as the ſhores or parts lying over againſt us.

Sir Edward Coke hath ſet down the record itſelf at large in French, which I ſhall not, for brevity's ſake, here repeat, but only give my reader an extract of it in Engliſh. Co.4.inſt. f. 14. 21, 43.

---- Do

--- Do declare, *That the kings of England by reason of that realm time out of mind have been in peaceable possession of the soverëign dominion of the sea of England, and of the islands situate in it, by ordering and establishing laws, statutes, and countermands of arms, and vessels, otherwise furnished than for merchandizing, and by taking security, and giving protection in all cases needful; and by the ordering all other things, requisite for the maintaining of peace and right amongst all other people, as well of other signiories as of their own passing thro' the same.*

Co.4.inst. 144. The laws of Oleron, which (after the Rhodian laws were antiquated) have now near 500 years been received by all the christian world, for regulating sea affairs, and deciding of maritime controversies, were first declared by our king Richard, at his return from the Holy Land, and by him caused to be published in the isle of Oleron, as belonging to the dutchy of Aquitain.

To these let me add, the recognition or acknowledgment of sea dominion of the kings of England, made by the Flemings, in an embassy to our king Edward the second, when the ambassadors of Robert earl of Flanders, complaining of their goods being taken at sea, and imploring remedy of the king of England; they said more than once, that they were taken upon the English sea, towards the parts about Crauden, within the power of the king of England, and brought into England; but that it appertained to the king of England; to take congnisance of the crime; *For that he is lord of the said sea, and the aforesaid depradation was committed upon the aforesaid sea within his territory and jurisdiction;* which are the words of the record.

Rot. pat. 14 Ed. 2. Membran 26 in dorso.

## 2. *Granting License or liberty to foreigners to fish in the British seas.*

We find that a licence for fishing hath been obtained by petition from the kings of England.

Rot. Parl. 2. R. 2. part. 2. Art. 38. in Schedula. There is a clear testimony of this prerogative in a record of the 2 R. 2. concerning those tributes or customs, that were imposed in this king's reign upon all persons whatsoever, that used fishing in the sea. The words of the record are these in our English idiom.

Item,

Item, *To take of every fisher-boat that fisheth upon the sea of the said admiralty for herrings, of what burthen soever it be, for each week of every ton six-pence.*

Moreover, it appears by a record of king H. 6. that he gave leave particularly to the French, and very many other foreigners, for one whole year only (sometimes for six months) &c. *to go and fish throughout the seas at all times, and as often*, &c. But this leave was granted under the name even of a passport or safe conduct; yea and a proportion was prescribed to their boats, that they should not be above 300 tons.

Rot. Franciæ 38. H. 6. Membran. 9. & 14.

Licenses to fish in the British seas, have been also granted by H. 6. to the dutchess of Burgundy; to those of Brabant by E. 4. to Philip king of Spain by queen Mary, for the Hollanders to fish upon the North coasts of Ireland, for the term of twenty-one years, paying yearly for the same 1000 l. which was accordingly paid into the Exchequer of Ireland.

Moreover also, in our time (says the famous antiquary Mr. Selden) leave was wont to be asked of our admiral, for the Frenchmen to fish for Soals in the neighbouring sea, for king H. 4. of France his own table; as it is affirmed by such who have been judges of our admiralty, and commanders at sea of an ancient standing; yea, and that the ships of those French were seized, as trespassers upon the sea, who presumed to fish without this kind of license.

Lib 2. c. 21. Of the dominion of the sea.

Mr. Cambden in his discourse of Yorkshire, saith, that no stranger durst let fall a net into the sea, till he had obtained leave of Scarborough castle.

In the seventh year of the reign of king James, this right was asserted by proclamation, and all persons excluded from the use of the seas upon our coasts, without particular licence; the grounds for this exclusion you may see in the proclamation itself.

6 to Maii anno Domini 1609.

But it may be demanded, whether other princes have such right of receiving tribute for fishing, and other matters in other seas?

It is answered, that they have, and do at this day receive tribute of strangers. At Coole, the empress of Russia; and Wardlings and Sound, the king of Denmark; all the princes of Italy, bordering upon the seas do the like; as the Venetians in the Adriatique sea; the Genoese, in the Ligustique; the Tuscans, in the Tyrrhene; the pope, in that which is called the Churches Sea.

### 3. *Granting Licenses of safe Conduct to Strangers.*

Strangers (by the law and custom of the British seas) either in coming to England, or going to any other place (without so much as touching upon any of his majesty's dominions) have used to take safe conducts, and licenses of the kings of England, to secure, and protect them in their voyage or passage, of which facts we have clear testimonies on records.

Rot. Franciæ 5 H. 4. membr. 11. Our Henry the fourth granted leave to *Ferrando Urtis de Sarachione*, a *Spaniard, to sail freely from the Port of* London, *through our Kingdoms, Dominions, and Jurisdictions, to the Town of* Rochel.

It is manifest (says Selden) that in this place, our dominions and jurisdictions, do relate to the sea flowing between.

5 H. 4. Membr. 14. When Charles the sixth, king of France, sent ambassadors to Robert the third king of Scots, to treat about the making a league; they upon request made to H. 4. obtained pass-ports for their safe passage and *Præter-Navigation, Par touz nos povoirs, destrois et signiories, per Mere, et per Terre*, that is, through all our powers, streights, and signiories, as well by sea as by land.

It is (says Selden) worthy of observation, that these kind of letters for safe conduct and passage, were usually superscribed and directed by our kings to their governors of the sea, admirals, vice-admirals, sea-captains; to wit, the commanders appointed by the king, to protect his territory by sea, whereas notwithstanding, we find no mention at all of any such commanders, in those pass-ports of that kind, which were granted heretofore by the French king, to the king of England, when he was to cross over into France. Letters of that kind were given to our Edward the second, by king Philip the long, superscribed only thus: *Philip by the grace of God king of* France; *To our Judges and Subjects greeting.* But the reason is evident, why the king of England was wont to direct his letters to his commanders

Rot. Clauf 13 Ed. 2. numb 7. in dorso.

commanders of the sea, and the French king at that time only to his judges, and subjects in general. Because the king of England had his sea-commanders throughout this whole sea, as lord of the same; and therefore when he crost over, it was not reasonable that the French king should secure him by sea, it being within the bounds of the English territories. To these authorities, I shall add but one more, which is this; John king of Sweden, in that letter of his sent to queen Elizabeth in the year 1587. desired leave for Olavus Wormæus, a Swede, to carry merchandise into Spain, acknowledging that he must of necessity *Maritima Reginæ ditiones pertransire, pass through the sea-dominions of the Queen*, which are the very words of the letter, in sir Robert Cotton's library.

These forementioned authorities do sufficiently assert on the behalf of the kings of England, the dominion and possession of the sea, from that leave of preter-navigation or passage, which hath been granted by them to foreigners.

4. *Imposing and receiving Tributes or Customs, for the Guard of the* English *Sea.*

Concerning the tributes or customs that were wont to be imposed, paid and demanded for the guard and protection of the English sea, there are very many ample, ancient testimonies before and since the reign of the Normans; but I shall content my self with one or two.

It is manifest, that the tribute first exacted in the reign of Ethelred by Anlaff the third, and afterwards imposed in the time of the English Saxons, for the guard of the sea, which was called Danegeldt, was wont now and then to be paid heretofore under the Norman kings.

It was paid in the reigns of William 1. William 2. H. 1. and king Stephen also. And Roger Hoveden saith expresly, that it was usually paid, untill the time of king Stephen. Annal. Parl. 1. p. 276.

In the parliamentary records of king R. 2. we find that a tribute or custom was imposed upon every ship that passed through the northern admiralty (that is, in the sea stretching it self from the Thames mouth, all along the eastern shore of England, towards the north-east,) for the pay and maintenance of the guard, or protection Rot. Parl. 2. R. 2. part 2. Art. 38. in Schedulâ.

protection of the sea; nor was it imposed only upon the ships of such merchants as were English, but also by the same right in a manner upon those of any foreigners whatsoever, no otherwise than if a man that is owner of a field, should impose an annual rent for the liberty of thorowfare, or driving cattle, or cart through his field. Payment was made at the rate of six pence a tun, upon every vessel that passed by.

Vide more of these matters in Mr. Selden's Mare Clausum, lib. 2. c. 15.

### 5. *Prescribing Limits to Foreigners that are at enmity with each other.*

Another evidence of the sea-dominion of great Britain is drawn from the laws and limits usually set by our kings in the sea, to such foreigners as were at enmity with each other, but in amity with the English.

About the beginning of the reign of James king of England the rest of the christian world was every where at peace, but the war waxed hot betwixt the spaniard and the states of the united provinces by which means it happened, that both those parties, being in amity with the English, did infest one another with mutual and very frequent depredations in the English seas; touching the lawfulness of these depredations divers questions arose amongst the king's officers, in the court of admiralty; our king following the examples of his predecessors, did as lawful sovereign, and moderator of the seas, set forth a proclamation, appointing certain limits upon the English coasts, within which he ordained there should be safe riding for both parties, with safe passage; yea, and declared that he would give equal protection to both in such manner, that within these limits, neither might the Spaniards use any hostility against the united Netherlands, nor those against them, nor the subjects of any nation whatsoever against those of another, without incurring his displeasure.

Procl. 1. Martis 2. Jac. an. 1604. in Rot. Pat. 2. Jac. Regis part 32.

Vide more in Selden's Mare Clausum lib. 2. c. 22.

6. *The*

### 6. *The ſtriking of the Top-ſails, by every Ship of any Foreign Nation whatſoever, if they ſail near the Kings Ships.*

It is affirmed by all that are uſed to the ſeas, as a fact indiſputable, that this intervenient law, or cuſtom of ſtriking ſail, hath been very uſual to the Engliſh and other nations; and that it is very ancient, and received for near 600 years, appears by the following record at Haſtings, a town ſituate upon the ſhore of Suſſex. It was decreed by king John (in the ſecond year of his reign, or of our lord 1200) with the aſſent of the peers; that if the governor or commander of the kings navy, in his naval expeditions *ſhall meet any Ships whatſoever by ſea, either laden or empty, that ſhall refuſe to ſtrike their ſails at the command of the kings governor, or admiral, or his lieutenant, but make reſiſtance againſt them which belong to the fleet; that then they are to be reputed enemies if they may be taken, yea, and their ſhips and goods be confiſcated as the goods of enemies. And that, though the maſters or owners of the ſhip ſhall alledge afterwards, that the ſame ſhips and goods do belong to the friends and allies of our lord the king. But that the perſons which ſhall be found in this kind of ſhips, are to be puniſhed with impriſonment at diſcretion for their rebellion.*

It was accounted treaſon (ſays our Selden) if any ſhip whatſoever had not acknowledged the dominion of the king of England in his own ſea, by ſtriking ſail.

To be ſhort, that the ſtriking of ſails is done, not only in honour of the Engliſh king, but alſo in an humble recognition and acknowledgment of his ſovereignty and dominion in the Britiſh ſeas, is preſumed a point out of queſtion. Sure the French cannot doubt of it, who by ſuch a kind of ſtriking, would have had themſelves heretofore acknowledged lords of our ſea, but in vain; that is to ſay, they were much overſeen in the former age, in ſetting forth two edicts, or ordinances, to acquire and ratifie ſuch a kind of ſtriking ſail to themſelves by all foreigners, as they were in ſo raſhly challenging the ſea-dominion of the king of England.

Vide edicts in Mr. Selden's Mare Clauſum Lib. I. c. 18. &. lib. 2. c. 26.

To

To these four special marks of sea-dominion, I will add the testimonies in our law-books, and the most received customs by which the sea-dominion of the king of England, is either asserted or admitted.

It must be acknowledged that some of the ancient authors of our law, after they had read through the civil law also, were so strict, in following those determinations word for word, which they found concerning the sea in that law, that when they treated *de Acquirendo Rerum Dominio*, of the manner of acquiring the dominion of things, they transferred them into their own writings. From thence it is, that Mr. Bracton saith, *Lib.* 1. *de rerum divisione c.* 12. *nu.* 5. & 6. *By the law of nature all these things are common, running water, the air and the sea, and the shores of the sea as accessories or dependants of the sea. Also if buildings be raised in the sea, or upon the shore, they become theirs that build them by the law of nations*; and a little after, *a right of fishing is common to all in haven, and in rivers.* But this very man afterwards lib. 2. c. 24. nu. 2. &. 5. f. 56, & 57, says, that by the kings grace and favour, *were exempted from paying tolls and customs, throughout the whole kingdom of* England *in the land, and in the sea, and throughout the whole kingdom both by land and by sea.*

Rot. Par. 51 H. 3. memb.11. A freedom was granted from some payments to the citizens of London, *throughout the whole kingdom, as well by sea as by land.*

Of purprestures (says Bracton) made upon our lord the king, either on land or on the sea, or in sweet waters, either within the liberties or without, or in any place whatsoever; by which words of Bracton is is recognized the dominion of the sea to be as much the right of the king, as the land.

Robert Belknap, one of R. 2. his judges tells us, that the sea is subject to the king, as a part of his English kingdom, or of the patrimony of the crown. His words in the Norman tongue run thus; *La Mere est del Legeans del Roy, come de son Corone d' Angleterre.* He addeth to his words (says Selden) in a remarkable way, *as belonging to the crown of England, or as, belonging to the royal patrimony of England*, to the end that no man might question, whether the sea belonged to the

the king by the right of the kingdom of England, or of the dutchy of Normandy, or of any other province in France.

Another alſo, that wrote in the reign of H. 3. ſaith, that of the old cuſtom of the realm, as the lord of the narrow (that is to ſay the Britiſh) ſea is bound to ſcour the ſea of pirates, and ſo it is read of the noble king Saint Edgar, that he ſcoured the ſea of pirates. St. German in his Doct. & Stud. lib. 2. c. 51.

To conclude; upon the authorities that I have here produced, to prove his majeſty's ſea-dominion, was grounded the declaration of that long parliament, *Anno* 16 and 17. Car. 2. which was in the preamble of their act thus: that the equipping and ſetting out to ſea of a royal navy, is for the preſervation of his majeſty's ancient and undoubted ſovereignty in the ſeas.

---

## 23. Prerogative.

*The king is ſole lord of all navigable rivers.*

THOUGH the king permits his ſubjects, for their eaſe and conveniency, to have common paſſage upon all navigable rivers; yet he hath as well the ſole intereſt, ſoil, ground and piſchary, as the care to redreſs all nuſances and obſtructions in ſuch ſtreams that are any impediment to navigation and paſſage, to and from the ſeas.

In proof of this prerogative, theſe authorities are producible:

It is found by commiſſion, that the river of Lee, which runneth from Ware to Waltham, and to London, is the high ſtream of the king. Dyer 117. a.

H. 8. Granted to *ſtrange-ways*, *totam libertatem piſcariam*, called the fleet in Abbots-bury, which is a bay, or creek in the ſea. Co. lib. 7. le caſe de Swannes.

The commiſſion of ſewers, that was awarded by the king, by virtue of his prerogative royal, before any ſtatute made in ſuch caſes, extends not only to the walls, and banks of the ſea, but alſo to navigable rivers. And it is recited in the ſtatute of 25 H. 8. c. 10. That the 25 H. 8. c. 10.

the king, by reason of his dignity and prerogative royal, ought to provide, that navigable streams be made passable.

27 H. 8. c. 16. Persons annoying the river Thames, by making shelves, casting dung, *&c.* incur a penalty of 5 *l.*

## 24. Prerogative.

*Chief lord of all ports and havens.*

THE king, by virtue of his prerogative royal, hath the custody of the havens, and ports of this island, being the very gates of the kingdom. He only in his royal function, is trusted with the keys of these gates; he alone therefore hath power to shut and to open them, when, and to whom, he in his princely wisdom shall see good.

Davy's Reports, le case de customs, f. 9. b. le case de royal piscchary, 56. l. The king (says Sir Jon Davys) is guardian of all the ports and havens of the realm, which are *Ostia seu Januæ Regni*; and therefore the king is *Custos totius Regni.* He ought of right to save and defend his realm, as well against the sea, as against the enemies.

## 25. Prerogative.

*Power of granting letters of marque and reprisal.*

THIS privilege is incident to the imperial crown of England, for the advancement of trade and commerce; and therefore, if an English merchant happen to be injuriously deprived of his goods by foreigners, and cannot obtain justice abroad, the king can grant letters of marque or reprisal to the party thus wronged, to redress himself out of the merchandizes of any subject of that country, to which the despoilers do belong.

The authority for proof of this prerogative is this:

The

The law of marque in ſome records, is called *jus regium*, becauſe by this prerogative the king, doth his liege's right: as in the parliament holden in 11 H. 4. John Cowley of Bridge-water, in his petition, prayed the king, that he might take marque or repriſal of all French goods (having no ſafe conduct of the king) to a certain value, for certain his ſhips and other goods taken by the French, in the time of the truce. The anſwer of the king was, that upon ſuit made to the king, he ſhould have ſuch letters requiſitory as are needful, and if the French king refuſe to do him right, the king will then ſhew his right. Co. 2. inſt. f. 205. on weſt. 1. c. 23.

*Vide* more, touching letters of marque. 27 E. 3. c. 17. 4 H. 5. c. 7.

---

## 26. Prerogative.

### *Power of granting licenſes to go beyond the ſeas:*

THOUGH by the law of nature every man hath his liberty to leave his native country, and to go whither he liſt; yet the rule of natural equity is to be obſerved with us, as in former times, amongſt the Romans, *viz*, *That it is not lawful, if prejudicial to the public intereſt*, according to the ſaying of Proculus, *Non id quod privatim intereſt unius ex ſociis ſervare ſolet, ſed quod ſocietati expedit.* Jus peregrinandi.

The authorities produced in proof of this prerogative are theſe:

Britton perſonating the king, ſpeaks thus, *Nul grand ſeignior, ne chivalier de noſtre realm, ne doit prender chemin ſans conge noſtre, car iſſint poet le realme remainer diſgarnie de forte gent.* c. 123. Co. Lit. 130. b.

In the tenth year of H. 2. it was declared, that it is not lawful for any arch-biſhops, biſhops, and other perſons to depart out of the realm without the king's leave; which although they have obtained, yet were notwithſtanding to ſecure the king, neither in their going, or returning, or ſtaying, to practice any thing prejudicious to his ſtate or perſon. Co. 3. inſt. 178.

Dyer, 128. b. If the king ſends a ſpecial command, under the privy ſeal or great ſeal, to any of thoſe that are in *partibus tranſmarinis*, and have gone out of the realm without licence, that they return into the realm by a day certain, under a penalty, *&c.* And if they refuſe to come, their lands and chattels ſhall be ſeized to the uſe of the king for the contempt.

The civil law joins hands with our law in this point of prerogative; *Edixit omnibus ſenatoribus* (ſays Dion of Auguſtus) *nequis eorum peregrinaretur extra Italiam injuſſu ſuo.*

---

## 27. Prerogative.

### *Power of granting liberties and franchiſes.*

Jus privilegiorum concedendorum. THOSE things that we term royal privileges, liberties and franchiſes, as hundreds, leets, wrecks, waifes, ſtrays, fairs, markets, park, warren, deodans, conuſance of pleas, and the like, may be (though appendant to the crown) ſeparated from it, and transferred to the ſubject, by the ſpecial grace of his majeſty, from whom, and his royal predeceſſors, kings and queens of England, all thoſe fore-mentioned liberties, with divers others, now in the hands of ſubjects; were at firſt derived.

In proof of this ſame prerogative, theſe authorities are offered:

Bracton, lib. 2. c. 24 num. 2. *Ea quæ dicuntur privilegia licet pertineant ad coronam à corona ſeparari poſſunt & ad privatas perſonas transferri, ſed de gratia ipſius regis ſpeciali.*

39 H. 6. 40. a. The king can grant to a man a charter of exemption, that he ſhall not be put on juries.

Co. lib. 12 the preſident and council of the North. The king by his letters patents, can grant to ſuch a corporation, in ſuch a town, *Tenere placita realia perſonalia & mixta.*

Co. lib. 11 87. It is not lawful for any man to erect a park, chaſe, or warren, without a ſpecial licenſe from the king, who is *pater patriæ*, and head of the commonwealth.

*In hoc rex Anglorum* (ſays Cowel) *legibus eſt ſuperior, quod privilegia pro arbitrio ſuo, dum tertio non injurioſa, perſonis ſingulis vel etiam municipiis aut collegiis concedere poſſit.* Caſe de Monopolies Co.2. inſt. 190. Inſt1.2.5.

---

## 28. Prerogative.

### *To the king belongs the cuſtody of Idiots and Lunaticks.*

IF we look into the laws of nature, we ſhall find that none are capable of dominion, but thoſe that have the exerciſe of ratiocination; however human laws have introduced a cuſtom in favour of Idiots, Lunaticks, and the like, ſo that they now are capable to have and enjoy, though not to order and diſpoſe of their properties; the diſpoſal of their properties belongs unto the king, who hath the ſupreme care of all his ſubjects in general, to defend their perſons and eſtates, from all manner of violence, uſurpation and oppreſſion, *a multo fortiori*, it is a duty in the king to defend and protect the properties and perſons of thoſe that are natural fools and madmen. Cura amentium.

In proof of this prerogative take theſe authorities:

The king by his prerogative, ſhall have the cuſtody of the lands of Idiots, finding them and their families neceſſaries, *&c.* and after the death of ſuch Idiots, rendering the eſtates to the right heir. 17 E. 2. c. 9 & 10.

This is by Statute; and by the Common-law, the king has the cuſtody of the body, goods and chattels of Idiots, after office found; but we muſt here make a diſtinction; for if a perſon hath once underſtanding, and becomes a fool by chance or misfortune, the king may not have cuſtody of him. And with reſpect to Lunaticks properly ſo called, the king hath only the *guardianſhip* of their lands, but not the *cuſtody* of their lands or bodies.

The eſtates and perſons of Idiots and Lunaticks, are by the law intruſted to the king. Hob. Rep Colt. and Glover verſus biſhop of

If an Idiot (ſays Coke) make a feoffment in fee, he ſhall in pleading never avoid it, by ſaying that he was an

Coventry and Litchfield, 155. Co. Lit. 247. a. an Idiot, at the time of the feoffment, and so hath been from his nativity, but upon an office found, the king shall avoid the feoffment for the benefit of the Idiot, whose custody the law giveth the king.

---

## 29. Prerogative.

*To a thing that may be of profit to the common people, the king can charge them without assent of the commons.*

THOUGH the king (whose authority over his subjects is not only royal but politic) can neither change laws, nor charge his subjects with subsidies, &c. without their consent, yet his majesty can charge them at his pleasure, with such things as may be of profit and benefit to the common people.

As for instance:

Co. lib. 12 f. 33. Le case de customs. 13 H. 4. 14. b. Cro. 1 part Heddy, v. Wheeler. 559.

The king may for the benefit of the subject, make an imposition or toll, within the realm, to repair highways, bridges, and to make walls for defence.

The king may grant a fair, and that toll shall be paid, although it be a charge upon the subject, because his subjects have benefit and ease by such fairs.

*Vide* more, 40 E. 3. 17. b. 18. a. 13. H. 4. 14. b.

---

## 30. Prerogative.

*Nothing that is incident to the crown shall pass from it, without express and determinate words.*

TO make men watchful in their affairs, and to put a period to many questions, about the construction of words; it is most agreeable to reason, that every man's words should be taken strongest against

against himſelf; but this rule hath its exception in reference to the king, whoſe words ſhall always be taken moſt advantagious for himſelf; becauſe the king is the ſole conſervator of the law, which is the commonwealth, and becauſe he is the ſupreme head, the law hath a more favourable eye to his rights, and will not permit any of them to paſs from the crown without expreſs and determinate words. As for example:

If the king grant all amerciaments, royal amerciaments do not paſs. 2 H. 7. 7. a.

The fine *pour congè d' accorder*, doth belong to the king, in ſo high a degree of prerogative, that it paſſes not by his general grant of all fines. Co. 2. Inſt 512.

It is adjudged, that by the grant of all mines in ſuch a ſoil, although that the grant be *ex certa ſcientia & mero motu*, mines royal of gold and ſilver ſhall not paſs; but the words [Soil and Mines] ſhall be taken in a common ſenſe, and to a common intent; but to have them paſs from the king, they ought to have ſpecial words. Co. lib. 1. Alton-wood's caſe. Davy's reports le caſe de cuſtoms. f. 17.

The king grants to me the chattels of ſelons and fugitives; for what offences ſoever, I ſhall not have the goods of one that ſtands mute: for theſe are forfeits for contempt, and this grant ſhall be taken ſtrictly, becauſe it ruſheth upon the king's prerogative. 8 H. 4. 2.

---

## 31. Prerogative.

### *Power of Denizating Aliens.*

THE law eſteemeth denizating of Aliens a point of high prerogative, annexing it individually to the ſacred perſon of the king, who by virtue of this royal preheminence, can make letters of denization, to whom, and how many he pleaſeth, enabling them to ſue in any action real or perſonal, and can make them capable of enjoying the laws, liberties, and inheritances of this realm, in ſuch ſort, as any natural born ſubject. Jus denizandi.

In proof of this prerogative, theſe authorities are offered:

A Den-

A Denizen is one that is infranchised by the king's letters patents, by which the king doth grant unto him, *Quod ille in omnibus reputetur, habeatur, teneatur, & gubernetur, tanquam ligeus noster infra dictum Regnum nostrum Angliæ oriundus, & non aliter, nec alio modo.*

The king may make a particular denization, as he may grant to an Alien, *Quod in quibusdam Curiis suis Angliæ, audiatur ut Anglicus, & quod non repellatur per illam exceptionem quod sit Alienigena. & natus in partibus, transmarinis*, to enable him to sue only.

The king can denizate an alien for life, in tail, or upon condition subsequent or precedent.

Civil law: *Antoninus pius multis é peregrinis Jus Romanæ Civitatis dedit.* Those that were aliens of another nation, were received into the Roman album, and made citizens of Rome.

---

## 32. Prerogative.

### *Right of Tribute.*

TRIBUTE is only due to him, in whom resides the superiority majestatical, and therefore a prohibitation to pay it to Cæsar, is an usurpation on sovereign power; and if there be a refusal to render it, 'tis an affront to God, and a violation of humane laws; for tribute and customs are due to his majesty by the law of God, the law of nations, and by the laws of the realm.

#### 1. *By the Law of God.*

St. Paul speaking of the higher powers, enjoineth subjects, to render to all their dues, tribute to whom tribute, custom to whom custom, and this injunction is grounded upon good authority; for we find that our blessed Saviour himself taught, that we are to render to Cæsar the things that are Cæsar's.

2. By

### 2. *By the law of Nations.*

Cicero in his epistles tell us, that *Imperium sine vectigalibus nullo modo esse potest. Neque Quies* (says *Tacitus*) *gentium sine Armis, neque Arma sine stipendiis, neque stipendia sine Tributis habere queunt.*

### 3. *By the Laws of the Realm.*

It is (says Plowden in his commentaries) the office of the king, to preserve his subjects in peace, and their preservation doth consist, in the due execution of the laws, and in armour to defend them against all hostility; now armour cannot be had, nor justice maintained without treasure, and no treasure without tribute and customs; hence it is, that in all cases where the king is put to expences, in discharge of his royal office, for the protection of the subject; the law yieldeth out of the thing protected some profit towards the maintenance of that charge, as for the upholding of courts of justice, the law giveth the king fines, and the like; for the safety of merchants upon the seas, customs, prisage, butlerage, tunnage and poundage, are to the king always allow'd to wage war with a foreign enemy, and to suppress rebellion, and insurrections at home; the king in parliament may levy aids and subsidies, but without the royal assent and authority, the order of both or either houses of parliament for the levying of taxes, are against the fundamental laws of the kingdom, and so 'tis declared in an act made in the thirteenth year of Charles 2d. Plowd. Com. Le. Case de Mines. 13. Car. 2. cap. 1.

Agreeable to this usage are the rules of the imperial law.

*Vectigalia sine Imperatorum præcepto, neque Præsidi, neque Curatori, neque Curiæ constituere nec precedentia reformare, & his vel addere vel diminuere licet.*

*Siquis Vectigalia imponere, absque illius Licentia ausus fuerit, Judicio Civili coercetur.*

*Non solent nova vectigalia, inconsultis principibus, institui; ergo & exigi aliquid, quod illicite possideatur, Competens Judex vetabit et id quod exactum videtur, si contra Juris Rationem extortum est, restitui Jubebit.* C. 4. 62 3.

33. Pre-

## 33. Prerogative.

*To the king the highest and most eminent love, legiance and reverence of all kinds is due.*

TO obey, revere, and love our prince, we are bound by the laws of God and man; disloyalty is an affront to the highest, who hath delegated sovereign power to kings and princes; for this cause Solomon advised us, to keep the king's commandment, and that, says he, in regard to the oath of God; but those subjects that have not taken the oath of allegiance, are as much bound, as if they had, allegiance being connatural, written by the pen of nature in the heart of every subject; it is therefore indelible, * *It cannot be forfeited, removed nor circumscribed within the four seas:* but subjects shall have obligations upon them of duty and loyalty in what part soever of the world they shall inhabit, and as their love and legiance flows from nature, so it ought to be in the highest degree of affection, beyond all other relations, yea life itself; for the public concerns were ever by loyal hearts preferred before any private interest; and therefore unto us, he necessarily must be dearer, from whom floweth the whole unity, and universal weal of the realm, His most excellent majesty being the pillar † that supports, the star that guides the ship of the commonwealth, the *spiritus vitalis* by which we subsist: for on his life depends the laws, the liberties, the properties, together with the glory of the English nation.

Co. 2. inst. on the stat. of Marleb. c. 10.

*Jus summe fidelitatis. Honora patrem,* is a precept of the moral law, which doubtless doth extend to him that is *Pater patriæ.* Co. lib. 7. Calvin's case. *Principi summi rerum arbitrium dii dederunt, subditis obsequii gloria relicta est.* Tacitus.

* Co. lib. 7. Calvin's case, *Ligeantia naturalis nullis claustris coercetur, nullis metis refrænetur, nullis finibus premitur. Vide* Co. Lit. 129. a. 13. Eliz. Dyer 330 b. Dr. Story's case. Cod. 10. 38. 4. D. 50. 1. 6.

† Alexander in Curtius is called *Macedoniæ Columen & Sydus.*

To

To study therefore the preservation of the king's person, to defend to the utmost his crown and dignity, against all violators of royal majesty, self-love (if not ‡ bounden duty) should prompt all subjects whatsoever.

The authorities offered in proof of this prerogative are these:

In doing homage to any subject, this clause always ought to be added (*salve le foy, que jeo doy a nostre seignior le Roy)* both because there is (says Sir Edward Coke) *homagium ligeum*, which is due to the king only, and also because he is sovereign lord over all. Lit. sect. 85, 86, 87.

And therefore, the reason a tenant is not sworn in doing his homage to his lord is, because no subject is sworn to another subject, to become his man of life, and member; but to the king only, and that is called the oath of allegiance. Co. Lit. 68. b.

Where the king is party, one shall not challenge the array for favour, *&c.* because in respect of his allegiance, he ought to favour the king more. Co. Lit. 156. a. 4 H. 7, 8. a.

To the king (says Coke) the highest and most eminent honour, legiance, and reverence of all kind is due. Co. Lit. 64. b.

To this prerogative, both Cicero and Seneca, give their attestation.

The former thus: *Est antiquior parens quam is, qui, ut aiunt, creaverit majori profecto quam parenti debetur gratia.* The king is Pater patriæ.

‡ That it is our duty, appears by the law of nature, the law of God, and the laws of the realm. 1. By the law of nature; Seneca of the emperor, *Somnum ejus nocturnis excubiis muniunt, circumfusique defendunt, incurrentibus periculis se opponunt: nec hæc vilitas sui est, aut dementia, pro uno capite tot millia accipere ferrum ac multis mortibus unam animam redimere, &c. Plutarc. Primum virtutis opus est, servare servantem cætera.* 2. It appears in the laws of God, 2 Sam. c. 21. v. 16, 17. cap. 23. v. 15. 16. cap. 18. v. 3. 3. In our law, it is our duty, as appears in 11 H. 7. c. 1, 18 and 19 H. 7. c. 1. Co. lib. 7. Calvin's case. Co. Lit. fol. 69. b. And in the statutes of 1 Eliz. c. 3. and 1 Jac. c. 1. The lords and commons in parliament promised to assist and defend the royal majesty, with expence of lives and fortunes.

The latter so, *Princeps regesque & quicunque alio nomine sunt tutores status publici, non est, mirum amari ultra privatas necessitudines, nam si sanis hominibus, publica privatis potiora sunt, sequitur ut is quoque charior sit, in quem respublica convertit.*

---

## 34. and last Prerogative.

### *Jus supplicationum.*

BEING informed sufficiently, that we are bound by our natural legiance, to obey and serve our sovereign lord the king, we may, I suppose, be easily perswaded, that it is our duty likewise to make prayers and supplications to God, for a blessing upon the sacred person and government of his majesty, to whom we owe, under God, all the peace, liberty, justice, property and prosperity we now enjoy.

By the statutes of 2 and 3 Ed. 6. c. 1. and 1 Eliz. c. 2. and 14 Car. 2. *Regis*, is ordained an uniformity of common-prayer and service in the church of England, in which office there are appointed prayers for the king, and this appointment is grounded on scripture, and the law of nature.

#### 1. *On Scripture.*

The Israelites shouted and said, *God save the king.* 1. Sam. 10, 24.

St. Paul exhorteth all Christians to make supplications, prayers, intercessions, and giving of thanks for all men, for kings, *&c.* 1 Tim. 2. 2.

#### 2. *On the Law of Nature.*

Calisthenes of king Alexander. in Curtius

*Ego seram immortalitatem precor regi, ut vita diuturna sit & æterna majestas.*

Pliny in his panegyrick to Trajan.

*Unum omnium votum est salus principis.*

Vivat Rex.

# POSTCRIPT.

HAVING apparented, that the imperial crown of England is, and was at all times *de jure*, (and I hope will be for ever *de facto*) inveſted of thoſe forementioned prerogatives, I ſhall preſume to detain the reader a few moments with a curſory view of ſome other privileges and preheminences, which were originally reſerved to the crown, and are part of the common-law of England; and they are ſuch as theſe:

1. The king is not bound to offer an acquittance to a ſubject, as he is obliged to offer to the king. 2 H. 7. 8. b. — *Acquittance.*

2. If the king make a leaſe for term of years, reſerving rent; if the rent be in arrear, he ſhall enter without any demand of the rent; ſo ſhall not a common perſon. 2 H. 7. 8. b. Co. lib. 4. Borough's caſe. Co. lib. 5. Knight's caſe. — *Demand of Rent.*

3. The king can grant a thing in a [illegible], and ſo ſhall not a ſubject. 2 H. 7. 10. a. 5 E. 4. [illegible] — *Choſe in Action.*

4. The grant of the king ſhall not enure to a double intent. 2 H. 7. 13. a. Co. lib. 1. 52. a. Alt[illegible]-wood's caſe. — *Double intent.*

5. Where a title appears from the king, the court *ex officio*, ought to award for him. And the king's title is not to be tried without warrant from the king, or the aſſent of the attorney-general. 12 H. 7. 12. a. Cro. 3. part. Yates v. Dryden. — *Title.*

6. The king may diſtrain for his ſervices, in other lands that are not holden of him. 5 H. 7. 39. a. 13 E. 4. 6. a. Co. 4. Inſt. f. 119. — *Diſtreſs.*

7. If money be paid to the king, and in his coffers, no judgment of reſtitution, as it ſhall in the caſe of a common perſon. 6 H. 7. 16. b. — *Money.*

Goods and chattels may go in ſucceſſion to the king, though they may not to any other ſole corporation. Finch, 83. — *Goods and Chattels.*

8. The king cannot be ſued, no action of covenant lies againſt him. 12 H. 7. 13. a. 2 H. 7. 3. b. 21 H. 7. 2. 4. — *Action.*

No prescription of time runs against the king, he is not within the statute of limitation of actions. Action lies not against the king, but a petition to him in chancery in its stead.

There are no costs allowed against the king.

Election both of court and action. 9. The king may sue in what court he pleases, and cannot be nonsuit, he may make choice of his action. He need not plead an act of parliament, tho' a subject must. Co. 4. Inst. 15, & 17. 12. H. 7. 21. b. 14. H. 7. 23. b. 14. E. 4. 5. 39. H. 6. 26.

Double count or plea. 10. The king shall not be said to make a double count or plea, as a subject may. 16. H. 7. 12. b.

Disseizing 11. The king cannot be disseized or put out of possession of things permanent, or of inheritance. No entry will bar him: and no judgement is ever final against him: and in the case of others, the king may issue a command to the judges not to proceed till he is advised where his right may be prejudiced. Doctor & Stud. Lib. 1. c. 8. 2. H. 4. 7. b. Co. lib. 6. Green's case. 21. E. 4. 2. 4. E. 4. 25. Cro. 2. part the King v. Champion f. 54. Cro 1. part the queen v. Vaughan.

Entire things. 12. Where the king comes to an entire thing by act of law as attainder, or by other act of law; he by his prerogative shall have the whole. Co. 3. Inst. 55. 8. E. 4. 4. Plowd. Com. 259. b. 7. E. 4. 7. Hobart's reports 127. Cro. 1. part f. 265.

No disseizor. 13. The entring upon me, by or without title, he shall not be accounted a disseizor, or abator. 3. E. 4. 25.

Action. 14. The king shall have every action, that another can have 22. E. 4. 48.

Toll, pontage. 15. The king shall not pay toll, pontage &c 35. H. 6 25.

Petition. 16. A disseizor infeoffs the king, the disseizee shall not enter. Sans petition 35. H. 6. 60, & 61.

The issue tryed at bar, or by Nisi prius. 17. The king may try his issue at the bar, or by Nisiprius, at his royal pleasure, Cro. 3. part. Southey v. Price 247.

Render en valur. 18. The king shall never render in value upon voucher. Cro. 3. part. f. 76.

19. If

Advowſon.

19. If the king have but two parts of an advowſon; yet he ſhall preſent alone, Hobart's Reports, chancellor of Cambridge. v. Walgrave f. 127.

Atturnment.

21. A grant to the king, or by the king to another, is good without atturnment, by his prerogative. Co. Lit. 309. b.

Kings debtor.

22. A common perſon ſhall not have execution againſt the king's debtor, untill agreement for the king's debt. Cro. 3 part. Stevenſon's Caſe.

Sole founder.

23. The king is ſaid to be founder, though another join with him in the foundation. Co. 2. Inſt. 68.

Clerks omiſſion.

24. The omiſſion of the clerk ſhall not prejudice the king. Cro. 3. part. 349.

Parol.

The king may preſent by parol. Cro. 2. part. v. 248.

Abatement of writs.

26. If the king bring an action, and the parties die, the writ ſhall not abate. Cro. 2. part. Dominus Rex. v. Web. 481.

Teſtimony.

The king's only teſtimony of any thing done in his preſence, is of as high nature and credit as any record: in all writs or precepts iſſued for the diſpatch of juſtice he uſeth no other witneſſes than himſelf, as *Teſte Meipſo*, &c.

King ſerved firſt.

27. Though a ſtatute be extended, yet after the king comes before the Liberate he ſhall be ſerved firſt. Hobart's Reports. Sheffield. v. Ratcliffe. 339.

Two titles concurring.

28. When the title of the king and a ſubject concur, the king's title ſhall be preferred. Co. lib. 9. Quicke's Caſe. lib. 4. Le Caſe de wardens. 55. a Plowden's Com. Hale's Caſe. Co. Litt. 30. b.

Protection.

29. The king may grant a protection to protect his debtor. Co. Litt. 131 b.

Plenarty.

31. Plenarty in a Quare impedit is no plea againſt the king. Co. Litt. 344. b. Co. 2. Inſt. 361.

Preſentation to a church.

32. If the king do preſent to a church, and his clerk be admitted and inſtituted; yet before induction, the king may repeal and revoke this preſentation. Co Litt. 344. b.

33. Any

Challenge 33. Any man may challenge for the king, shewing particular cause. Co. 2. Inst. 431.

Kings debt. 34. By order of the common law, the king for his debt had exemption of the body, lands, and goods of the debtor, Co. 2. Inst. f. 19.

Grant of a thing not in esse. 35. The king can grant a thing that is not in him, as he may grant, that I shall be discharged of a 15. granted at the next parliament. 6. H. 7. 5. a. 32. H. 6. 9. 35. H. 8. Dyer 56. b.

King deceived. 36. If the king be deceived in his grant, the grant is void, notwithstanding the words, *Ex Gratiâ speciali, ex certa Scientiâ*, and *ex mero motu*, which do imply bounty, knowledge, and done without suggestion. Co. lib. 6. Green's case, 29. b. Co. lib. 1. 43. b. 44. a 46. a. Alton-wood's case.

Privilege of cinque ports, &c. avail not against the king. 37. The privilege of parliament, of the cinque ports, or any other place doth hold between subject and subject; but no privilege or franchise, in case of treason, felony, the peace, or imprisonment, can be against the king; and therefore to dispute his commands is not to dispute the jurisdiction, but the power and prerogative of the king, and his courts at Westminster. Co. 4. Inst. 25. 215. Cro. 3. part. Soutley. v. Price 24. Cro. 2. part. Bourne's case. Cro. 1. part. Crispe v. Verral.

Kings palace. 38. The kings palace is a privileged place from all summons, and citations. Co. 3. Inst. 141.

To come to a conclusion; the law of England hath so much reverence and honour for our king, that it alloweth him (as God's vicegerent on earth) almost divine attributes, as,

1. Immortality; the king never dies, Co. Litt. 9. b. Co. lib. 6. le case de Souldiers. 27. a. Co. 3. Inst. f. 7.
2. Omnipresence; he is ever present in court, 1. H. 7. 13. b.
3. Perfection; the king cannot be said to be a minor, and in him the law will see no defect, negligence, or folly. Co. Litt. 43 ab Co. 4. Inst. 209, & 210.
4. Omniscience; *Rex omnia Jura habet in Scrinio pectoris sui.* Co. Litt. 99. a.

5. Truth

5. Truth and wiſdom; *Rex fallere non vult, falli autem non poteſt.*
6. Juſtice; the king can do no wrong. Co. Litt. 19. b. Co. lib. 1. 44. b. Alton-wood's caſe, Plowden's Com. 246.
7. Majeſty and ſupremacy.
8. Sovereignty and power.

And out of a dutiful reſpect to theſe ſuper-eminent and almoſt God-like attributes, it is the cuſtom of this realm as ſir Thomas Smith obſerves (lib. 2. c. 4.)

*That no man ſpeaketh to the prince, nor ſerveth at the table but in adoration and kneeling: all perſons of the realm be bare-headed before him: inſomuch that in the chamber of preſence, where the cloath of eſtate is ſet, no man dare walk; yea though the prince be not there, no man dare tarry there, but bare-headed.*

FINIS.

www.ingramcontent.com/pod-product-compliance
Lightning Source LLC
Chambersburg PA
CBHW030545270326
41927CB00008B/1526

* 9 7 8 3 3 3 7 2 7 2 0 9 8 *